CULTURES OF THE WORLD
Fiji

Cavendish
Square
New York

Published in 2020 by Cavendish Square Publishing, LLC
243 5th Avenue, Suite 136, New York, NY 10016
Copyright © 2020 by Cavendish Square Publishing, LLC

Third Edition

Library of Congress Cataloging-in-Publication Data

Names: NgCheong-Lum, Roseline, 1962- author. | Nevins, Debbie, author.
Title: Fiji / Roseline NgCheong-Lum, Debbie Nevins.
Description: Third edition. | New York : Cavendish Square, [2020] |
Includes bibliographical references and index. | Audience: Grades 6 and up.
Identifiers: LCCN 2018050567 (print) | LCCN 2018050799 (ebook) |
ISBN 9781502647450 (ebook) | ISBN 9781502647443 (library bound)
Subjects: LCSH: Fiji--Juvenile literature.
Classification: LCC DU600 (ebook) | LCC DU600 .N45 2019 (print) |
DDC 996.11--dc23
LC record available at https://lccn.loc.gov/2018050567

Writers: Roseline NgCheong-Lum; Debbie Nevins, third edition
Editorial Director, third edition: David McNamara
Editor, third edition: Debbie Nevins
Art Director, third edition: Alan Sliwinski
Designer, third edition: Jessica Nevins
Production Manager, third edition: Karol Szymczuk
Cover Picture Researcher: Alan Sliwinski
Picture Researcher, third edition: Jessica Nevins

CONTENTS

FIJI TODAY

FIJI—FOR MANY PEOPLE, THE VERY NAME CONJURES UP A FARAWAY, exotic paradise, one that hides a dark, dangerous secret. For others, it's a dream honeymoon or vacation destination. For the people who live there, of course, it's simply home. And all of these perceptions are correct, in some way.

Fiji is an island nation in the South Pacific Ocean, an archipelago of some 330 volcanic islands and low-lying atolls. White sandy beaches, shifting sand dunes, colorful coils of reefs teeming with marine life, and impenetrable rain forests all form part of its landscape. Though about 110 of the islands are inhabited, most of the population—87 percent—lives on one of the two largest islands, Viti Levu and Vanua Levu.

Fiji is far from just about anywhere. Aside from numerous other tiny Pacific islands, its closest neighbor is New Zealand, some 1,300 miles (2,000 kilometers) to the south. The air travel distance, from airport to airport, is even farther. But this isolation in the South Pacific did not prevent humans from finding these islands. As far back as 3500 BCE, seafaring people from Southeast Asia found their way there, and stayed.

Fijians sail with tourists in the shallow waters off of an uninhabited island.

Today, Fiji is a crossroads of cultures. The population includes indigenous Fijians, now called iTaukei; Indians, ancestrally related to India; Polynesians; Chinese; and Europeans. All lmore or less live side by side as separate groups. While calling Fiji their home, the migrant communities have each retained their ancestral religions, customs, and cultures.

There is one custom, however, that native Fijians have completely let go. Today, they laugh to even think of it. But there was a time, more than a century ago, when Fiji held a terrifying truth in its deepest, darkest heart: cannibalism! Among some tribal groups, it was customary to eat their enemies, particularly following a battle. Indeed, as this ancient tradition was discovered by Europeans, Fiji became a place of both fear and fascination. Nineteenth-century European sailors nicknamed Fiji "the Cannibal Isles" and were wary of landing there.

Today, that custom is (almost certainly) a thing of the past, and Fiji's connection to cannibalism has the opposite effect. It has become a tourist attraction of sorts. Souvenir shops sell handcrafted cannibal dolls made of coconut shells, and replicas of wooden forklike tools once used specifically for consuming human flesh.

Today's iTaukei Fijians are devoted Christians who naturally find that particular piece of their cultural history to be revolting. But they also understand that the old rituals and beliefs have to be understood within the context of their own realities. Not so long ago, Europeans justified the conquering and colonization of Fiji by labeling its people as uncivilized savages. This inherently racist attitude of cultural superiority fueled the entire expansion of the British Empire, of which Fiji was a part for about a century.

Today, Fiji is an independent nation with a thriving economy that depends greatly on tourism. Although it's still seen as a "developing nation," it's one of the most highly developed of the South Pacific islands. The 2018 United

Nations Human Development Index (HDI)—which evaluates countries' overall achievement in social and economic terms—rated Fiji as number 92 out of 189 nations (in which 1 is the highest level and 189 is the lowest). In 2018, Norway topped the list, and the African nation of Niger scored the lowest. To measure the vague concept of "human development," the HDI looks at a population's average life expectancy at birth, education level, and income level. Fiji's rating puts it in the category of "high human development." (For comparison, the United States is in the category of "very high human development."

Despite its relatively high standing, Fiji faces some serious problems. Among the most important are ethnic relations between iTaukei and Indians, government stability, poverty, and environmental concerns. All of these issues are discussed later in this book.

But Fiji has so many positive things going for it—its famously friendly and hospitable people, its natural beauty and abundant resources, and its return to democratic rule in 2016—that the future appears to bode well.

Saving turtles is an important part of Fiji's environmental work. The leatherback turtle, shown here, is the largest of the sea turtles, all of which are threatened in Fiji. The leatherback, however, is critically endangered. In 2009, the government set in place the first ten-year moratorium on hunting sea turtles.

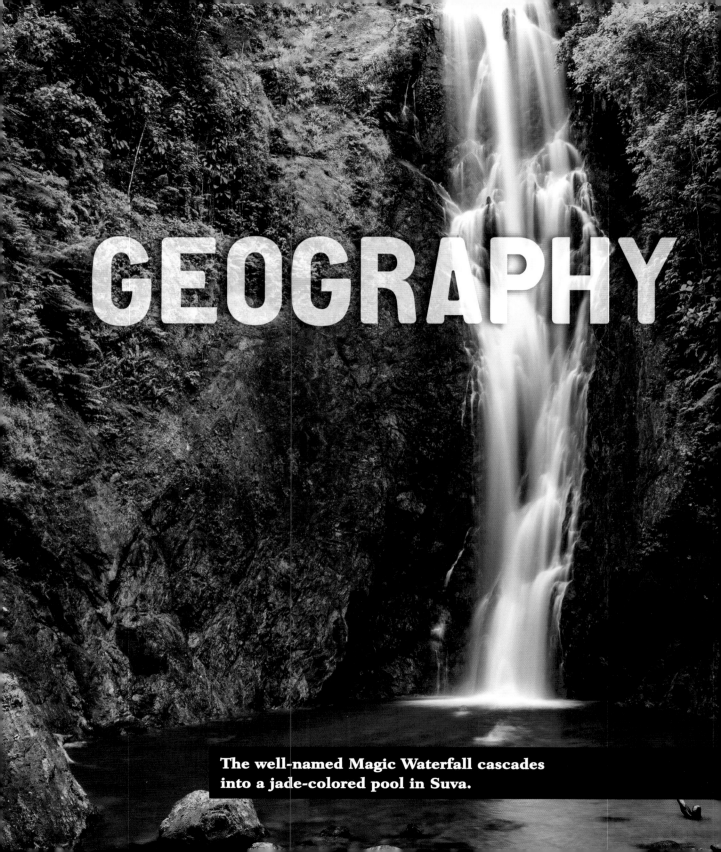

GEOGRAPHY

The well-named Magic Waterfall cascades into a jade-colored pool in Suva.

1

IF PRESENTED WITH AN UNLABELED map of the world, most people—aside from Fijians themselves, of course—might have a tough time picking out Fiji. Even if the search is correctly narrowed to the islands of the South Pacific, the task could be tricky, because there are many thousands of such islands. Some, like Fiji, are nations unto themselves; while many others are territories of other nations.

Sprawling across an area of about 501,800 square miles (1,300,000 square kilometers) in the fabled South Seas, the Fijian archipelago is made up of 332 islands, of which about one-third are inhabited. Hundreds of smaller islets exist as well, and some of them are also inhabited. Lying just north of the Tropic of Capricorn, the country is slightly larger than California and Nevada put together. Less than 1.5 percent of the area is land (7,056 square miles, or 18,274 sq km)—slightly smaller than New Jersey; the rest is open sea.

The 180° meridian passes through the islands. This imaginary north—south line is one of two lines of longitude that mark the boundaries of the earth's Western and Eastern Hemispheres. It's used as the basis for the International Date Line, which divides the world into today (on the west side) and yesterday (on the east side). However, it bends east to accommodate Fiji, so the country's time zone is not split into two days.

Fiji was once known as part of the "Cannibal Isles." Cannibalism existed there until Christian missionaries arrived in the mid-1800s.

Geographically, Fiji is a cluster of islands located in a larger group of islands called Melanesia, which is itself part of an even bigger region of islands called Oceania. Encompassing more than ten thousand Pacific islands, Oceania straddles Earth's equator, including islands in the North Pacific and others in the South Pacific. The region also spans both the Eastern and Western Hemispheres, which are divided by the 180° meridian.

As a name, the term was coined in 1812 by a French geographer. As a precise location, the region is loosely defined. Neither a continent nor a nation unto itself, it's called Oceania because it is the ocean that links its various parts together. Sometimes the definition includes Australia and, even less often, the Malay Archipelago. However, it always includes the regions of Micronesia, Melanesia, and Polynesia.

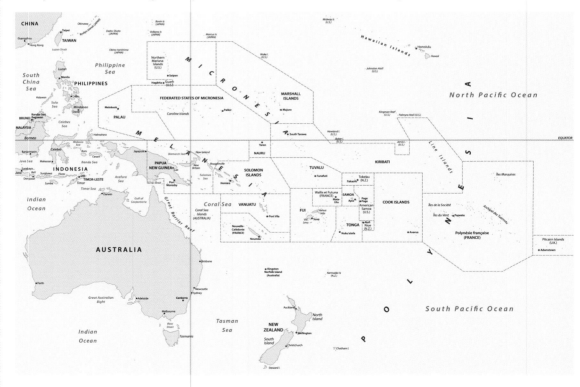

Fiji is the dividing point between the old divisions of Polynesia and Melanesia. It is now officially placed in Melanesia; geographically and culturally, however, it marks a blending of the two regions. To the east are the low coral atolls and volcanic islands of Polynesia. Moving west, the mountainous volcanic and continental islands of Melanesia arise.

The nearest large city is Auckland, New Zealand, which is located about 1,300 miles (2,092 km) to the south. Honolulu is five hours away by air, while Los Angeles is a ten-hour flight.

THE FIJIAN ARCHIPELAGO

Fiji is composed of two large islands, Viti Levu and Vanua Levu, ringed by groups of smaller islands. The archipelago surrounds the Koro Sea.

VITI LEVU The largest island is Viti Levu. Meaning "Big Fiji," it is the hub of the Fijian archipelago. It's about the same size as the Big Island of Hawaii, and slightly smaller than the state of Connecticut. Also the most developed island in the archipelago, Viti Levu is home to 70 percent of the Fijian people, who live mostly on its coastal perimeter, the rugged interior being sparsely populated. One peculiarity of this island is the astonishing contrast between the east and west halves. While the eastern side is lushly wet and green, the western part is dry and sun-baked. It is the western coast that most tourists visit and where large areas of sugarcane plantations are located.

Suva, the largest city and port, and the capital of Fiji, is set on the southeastern shore. The Nausori Highlands is a spectacular mountainous region in the central part of the island. Viti Levu is the site of the country's highest mountain, Mount Tomanivi, and its longest river, the Rewa. Off the east coast of Viti Levu is a small island, Bau. Formerly the indigenous capital, Bau is still the residence of the high chiefs of Fiji. Kadavu, the third largest island in Fiji, is located 62 miles (100 km) south of Suva. Rotuma, a Polynesian island set 440 miles (708 km) to the north of Suva, also belongs to Fiji. It has an area of 18 square miles (47 sq km).

VANUA LEVU The second-largest island, Vanua Levu, is about half the size of Viti Levu. Its name means "Big Land," and it is the homeland of about 17 percent of the total population. Much less developed than its bigger neighbor, the island is rugged and is surrounded by an extensive system of coral reefs. Volcanic in origin, the island has few beaches. Wide geographical contrasts are seen between the different regions. The interior is wild and mountainous, for example, while the western district is arid and sunburned. The southern coast is notched by several wide bays fringed with palms. Vanua Levu used to be the center of the copra, or coconut meat, trade, but today sugar cultivation is the most important industry, and large cane fields can be seen on the dry western and northern coasts.

THE LAU GROUP Made up of fifty-seven islands, this group lies to the east of Vanua Levu. Although scattered over more than 43,243 square miles (112,000 sq km), their total land area is only 188 square miles (487 sq km). The islands in the southern part of the group are closer to Tonga, a separate island nation, than to the Fijian capital, and they reflect quite a bit of their Polynesian endowment. Lakeba, a central island, is a meeting place between Fijians and Tongans, and it serves as the traditional political center of the whole group.

OTHER ISLANDS Taveuni is a large island to the southeast of Vanua Levu. It is notable for Mount Uluigalau, which lies on the 180° meridian, and the indigenous tagimaucia flower, which grows only here.

Lomaiviti, or Central Fiji, consists of seven large volcanic islands and a few small ones east of Viti Levu. Ovalau is separated from Viti Levu by 10 miles (16 km) of shallow sea. Levuka, on Ovalau, was the capital of Fiji until 1882. Situated at the foot of a steep bluff, it cultivates the ambience of a nineteenth-century whaling town.

The Yasawa Group is a crescent-shaped chain of islands to the northwest of Viti Levu, consisting of sixteen islands and numerous islets, all of volcanic origin. Since they are located on the leeside of Viti Levu, these small islands are dry and sunny all year round. As the Yasawas are only a hop away from

Coral reefs are underwater ecosystems mostly found in shallow tropical seas. A coral consists of polyps, which are soft living organisms that secrete a hard calcium carbonate exoskeleton similar to a seashell. Colonies of coral polyps are held together by the calcium carbonate, becoming a common skeleton that builds the reef. It takes billions of polyps thousands of years to produce a few square miles of reef.

Often called "rainforests of the sea," shallow coral reefs are some of Earth's most diverse ecosystems. They are natural habitats to more than 25 percent of all marine life and are among the world's most fragile and endangered ecosystems. If undisturbed, the coral continues to build on itself and grow in size. Millions of polyps live on top of the limestone remains of former colonies, creating the massive reefs. The color and shape of the coral depend on a number of factors, including the amount of light the coral receives and the quality of the seawater. Many reefs around the world have been damaged by human activity.

The waters off Fiji have some of the most beautiful coral reefs in the world. In fact, Fiji has been called the Soft Coral Capital of the World by enthusiastic divers. There are three types of reefs in Fiji—"fringing" reefs along the coastline, "barrier" reefs separated from the coast by a lagoon, and "atoll" reefs, which are circular or horseshoe-shaped. The Great Astrolabe Reef, Rainbow Reef, Great Sea Reef, and the Argo Reef in the Lau Islands are among the most famous coral reefs in Fiji. Protecting the precious reefs, while generating revenue from tourism and diving, is a difficult balancing act for the Fijian government.

Viti Levu's west-coast city of Nadi by a fast catamaran, they have become favorites with backpackers.

CLIMATE

Fiji enjoys a tropical maritime climate tempered by the southeast trade winds from May to October. The country experiences very slight temperature variations between the seasons. Summer lasts from October to March,

Debris lies around a house on Viti Levu, part of the destruction caused by Cyclone Winston.

with daytime highs of 85 degrees Fahrenheit (29 degrees Celsius) and high levels of humidity. Winter temperatures average 68°F (20°C). In general, temperatures are cooler at higher elevations, especially in the mountainous interior of the large islands. Most rain falls in the summer months. The average annual rainfall is 120 inches (305 centimeters). The western parts of the Fiji Islands receive virtually no rain from April to October.

Destructive hurricanes often batter this archipelago. The months of November to April are dubbed the hurricane season. Hurricanes develop from low-pressure centers near the equator. They usually reach their full force in latitudes such as Fiji's. Nevertheless, very destructive hurricanes are rare in Fiji. On average, Fiji experiences about two cyclones—severe tropical hurricanes—a year, much lower than other islands in the region. When a cyclone does hit, though, the wreckage is extensive, with storms causing millions of dollars in damage to towns, agriculture, and the tourist industry. In April 2018, the back-to-back cyclones Josie and Keni caused widespread flooding, downed trees and electrical lines, structural damage, and the deaths of several people. And in February 2016, Cyclone Winston, the most powerful storm in the country's recorded history, caused tremendous devastation.

PEAKS AND RIVERS

The larger islands are notably mountainous, rising abruptly from the shore to impressive heights. Most of them are of volcanic origin, as shown by the massive volumes of volcanic sediments and limestone deposits found. The highest peak in the country is Mount Tomanivi on Viti Levu. Formerly called Mount Victoria, it towers at a height of 4,341 feet (1,323 meters). Several other mountains rise to more than 3,000 feet (914 m).

Fiji also has many waterways. The longest river is the Rewa on Viti Levu, navigable for 81 miles (130 km) from its mouth. Other rivers on Viti Levu

THE LEGEND OF TAGIMAUCIA

The tagimaucia (Medinilla waterhousei) is one of Fiji's most beautiful wildflowers. Blooming in long, 12-inch (30-centimeter) bunches from late September to late December, the red flowers display a white interior with a small red center. They grow on a thick green vine bearing large green leaves. The plant grows only on the banks of Lake Tagimaucia, high in the mountains of Taveuni, and all attempts at transplanting it have failed. One of the most interesting features of the tagimaucia is that it comes with a beautiful legend.

A woman and her young daughter lived on a hill in Taveuni. One day, the little girl was playing when she should have been helping her mother do the housework. Despite her mother's repeated requests, she kept on playing. At last the angry mother hit her with the broom and ordered her to go away and never come back. The brokenhearted little girl ran away, crying. With tears rolling down her cheeks, she darted into the forest, not knowing where she was going. Blinded by her tears, she stumbled into a climbing plant hanging from a tree and became entangled in its vines. Unable to break free, she sobbed bitterly. As the tears fell, they changed into tears of blood. When her tears touched the stem of the vine, they turned into beautiful blood-red flowers.

At last the girl stopped crying and managed to set herself free. She ran back home to find that her mother had forgiven her, and they lived happily together ever after. Since that day, lovely red flowers have bloomed on the tagimaucia vine.

include the Sigatoka and Ba. Vanua Levu also has many rivers, although they are not as long as those on Viti Levu. The largest is the Dreketi River.

FLORA

Almost half of Fiji's land area is still covered with rain forest. Forested areas are found mainly in the high plateau regions. Rain forest species include the *dakua* and *yaka*, which are durable woods used to make furniture. These species are becoming rarer because replacement trees are not planted after excessive logging. There are several edible ferns in Fiji, known as *ota*. Another edible plant is the *nama*, or grape-weed, a seaweed that Fijians consider a delicacy. Other common edible plants in Fiji include food staples such as cassava, taro, and breadfruit.

Casuarina trees, pandanus, and coconut palms flourish in the dry coastal areas. Fiji has several species of pandanus, or screw pine, which are grown around villages. Screwpine leaves are used to thatch roofs and in weaving baskets and mats. Mangrove swamps cover the eastern coastlines, while dry grasslands are found in the western areas of the large islands. More than three thousand species of plants have been identified. One-third of them are native to Fiji, and there are about eight hundred species of plants found nowhere else in the world.

The most famous is the fuchsia-like tagimaucia, which grows on a single mountain ridge of Taveuni. It has red and white petals and bright green vines and leaves. The national flower of Fiji is the hibiscus. Introduced from Africa, it is commonly used for decoration and food, and in making dyes and medicines.

FAUNA

Fiji has scant indigenous wildlife. Most species were introduced to the islands by the first seafaring settlers about 3,500 years ago. One of the more interesting creatures is the mongoose, a ferret-like animal that preys on rodents. And Vitu Levu is the only known home of the world's second-largest insect, the giant Fijian long-horned beetle, whose body can grow to about 6 inches (16 cm) long.

Of the more than sixty species of birds, twenty-three are actually native to Fiji. The orange dove can be seen only on Taveuni. There are also six species of bats and a few remarkable lizards. The crested iguana is one of the rarest reptiles in Fiji. Discovered in the early 1980s on a tiny island off Vanua Levu, it is believed to have drifted from South America to Fiji. Some snakes also live in the Fijian archipelago. One of them, the banded sea krait, is three times more venomous than the Indian cobra. Marine life is varied and includes most species of tropical fish. The leatherback turtle, which can grow up to 7 feet (2.1 m), is a wholly protected species.

THE NEW AND OLD CAPITALS

Suva became the capital of Fiji in 1882, thanks to its wide harbor and fertile land. It is now the country's administrative and political center and its major port. Since becoming the capital, Suva has grown from two hundred to more than seventy thousand inhabitants, and the town is continually expanding. Much of today's waterfront sits on reclaimed land. Suva is a cosmopolitan city, with many churches, temples, mosques, and cultural centers. The University of the South Pacific and the fascinating Fiji Museum are located there.

Levuka, the first colonial capital of Fiji, teems with history and old-world charm. Sandalwood traders settled there in 1806, making Levuka the first European settlement in Fiji. The town prospered throughout the nineteenth century as sailors, whalers, and planters came ashore. Before the capital was moved to Suva, Levuka was a wild and lawless place. Today, Levuka is the site of many historical landmarks, including the Cession Site. A stone marks the spot where the deed granting Fiji to Britain was signed in 1874. The people of Levuka are mostly of mixed Fijian and European descent.

INTERNET LINKS

https://www.britannica.com/place/Fiji-republic-Pacific-Ocean
This online encyclopedia has information about the land, climate, animals, and plants of Fiji.

http://lntreasures.com/fiji.html
Living National Treasures' Fiji page provides links for info about and photos of all Fiji's endemic species.

https://www.lonelyplanet.com/fiji/taveuni/travel-tips-and -articles/diving-and-snorkelling-in-fiji/40625c8c-8a11-5710-a052 -1479d2763849
This article, with beautiful photos, focuses on snorkeling around some of Fiji's reefs.

https://www.nytimes.com/2017/02/01/world/asia/a-rare-pacific -islander-captivates-its-neighborhood.html
This article about the tagimoucia flower includes beautiful photos of the Fijian rain forest.

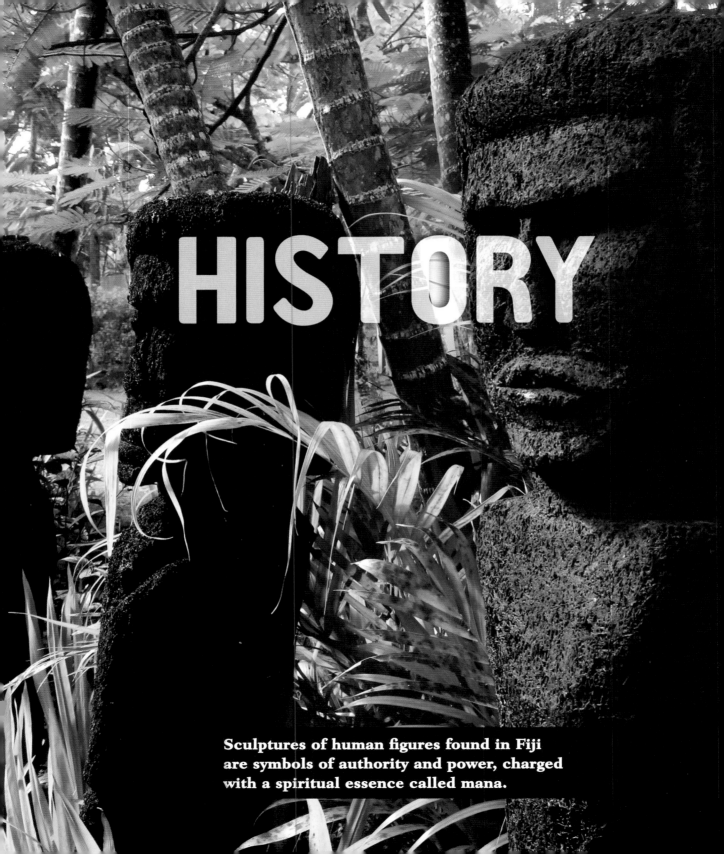

HISTORY

Sculptures of human figures found in Fiji
are symbols of authority and power, charged
with a spiritual essence called mana.

2

FIJIAN TRADITION CLAIMS THAT THE country was established by the legendary chief Lutunasobasoba, who arrived from Lake Tanganyika in Africa in a great canoe called Kaunitoni and landed on Viti Levu at Vuda Point. From there, he and his followers moved inland and settled the whole island.

Although no evidence exists to substantiate this story, many Fijian clans claim to be descendants of the first chief. Nevertheless, many anthropologists and linguists dispute that history, and suggest it was first promulgated by missionaries. Instead, most researchers hold that the first people to inhabit Fiji came from Southeast Asia, not from Africa. Evidence does, however, confirm that Fijian settlement is ancient and sophisticated. Spanning more than three thousand years, Fijian history is sometimes mysteriously clouded and at other times highly tumultuous.

THE EARLY INHABITANTS

The first known human settlement in Fiji dates from around 1050 BCE at Bourewa in southwest Viti Levu. Archaeological evidence indicates that the first settlers came from Papua New Guinea. The early Fijians were Lapita people, so called after a style of pottery found in coastal locations on many Pacific islands. Originating from Southeast Asia, the Lapita people were seafarers who, beginning 3,500 years ago, made their way quickly

The Polynesian peoples who settled Fiji were astonishingly good navigators: they sailed across huge stretches of the Pacific Ocean. Their elegant canoes were propelled by teams of rowing men. They might have sailed as far as Hawaii. Pots made in Fiji were found in Samoa and the Marquesas Islands, a distance of nearly 3,000 miles (4,828 km)!

through Melanesia and the Solomon Islands and across the western Pacific to reach Fiji, Tonga, and Samoa. They made intricate forms of pottery and were highly skilled in navigation and canoe building.

A second wave of settlers, from Melanesia, reached Fijian shores around 500 BCE. As the population grew, the inhabitants moved farther inland and turned to agriculture. Soon after, the Lapita people seem to have disappeared from Fiji, or were absorbed into the new culture.

Around 1000 CE, Polynesian peoples invaded from Tonga, resulting in large-scale wars. By the early thirteenth century, Fiji was a province of the Tongan Empire. A complex class structure evolved within the tribes, each headed by a hereditary chief. Considered a spiritual being, a chief enjoyed absolute power over his subjects, who lived in *mataqali* (mah-tang-GAH-lee), or extended family groups. Marriages between the tribes were a good way of making peace, but fierce tribal warfare was still very common.

THE WHITE MAN

The first reported sighting of Fiji by Western navigators was in 1643 by Dutchman Abel Tasman on his way to Indonesia. His descriptions of the treacherous Fijian waters kept others away for the next 130 years. In 1774, Captain James Cook visited the archipelago, stopping at Vatoa in the Lau Group. In 1789, Captain William Bligh passed between Viti Levu and Vanua Levu after the mutiny on the British merchant ship HMS *Bounty*. Although he was hotly pursued by the hostile indigenous people, he made detailed and accurate observations of the islands.

Not until the early nineteenth century did Europeans begin to show interest in Fiji. In 1804, a group of shipwrecked sailors discovered sandalwood on the southwest coast of Vanua Levu, and the forests of Fiji were quickly ravaged by the beachcombers, who were mainly from Australia. This popular scented wood was bought for $50 per cargo and sold to the Chinese for $20,000. Within ten years, all sandalwood resources were depleted.

In the 1820s, an aquatic animal, the bêche-de-mer, a type of sea cucumber used in Asia as food and folk medicine, brought the traders back to the archipelago. By the 1830s, Fiji was flooded with sailors from Australia, New

CANNIBALS!

By all accounts, the Fijian people were a savage and brutal lot. One of their most repugnant practices, reported by the early Europeans, was cannibalism. For many years, the islands were called the Cannibal Isles, and this foreboding reputation kept many Europeans away from Fijian waters.

Cannibalism was practiced in Fiji from about 2,500 years ago until the late nineteenth century. Prisoners of war, women captured while fishing, and shipwrecked sailors were invariably eaten. The worst fate that could be dealt to a captured enemy was to eat him. Eating a person meant destroying their spirit. Dead bodies were usually consumed on the battlefield, but live prisoners were taken back to

This sacred Fijian temple was a place where some groups of islanders performed cannibalistic rites.

the village and sacrificed to the local war god before being cooked and eaten on the god's behalf. In some cases, the victors' cruelty went so far as throwing the victims alive into the ovens, making them watch their body parts being eaten, or even forcing them to eat some of their own parts themselves.

Ratu (Chief) Udreudre, a nineteenth-century chief on Viti Levu, was reputed to have eaten 872 victims. To keep track, he would add one stone to a big pile for each person eaten. According to his son, he never shared any of his victims, setting aside the prime human flesh in a box so as not to lose any.

Among the more often told cannibal stories is that of the Reverend Thomas Baker. The Wesleyan Methodist missionary, whose task was to convert the people of Viti Levu, unfortunately offended the highlands people and was killed in July 1867. His flesh was shared among the neighboring villages and eaten. The only thing remaining of the missionary was a shoe, which is now exhibited in the Fiji Museum.

Zealand, China, the United States, and Europe. In return for processing bêche-de-mer for the foreigners, the Fijians gained access to tobacco, metal tools, clothes, and guns.

The availability of modern weapons provoked havoc among the warlike Fijians. The local population was further decimated by diseases brought in by the white men. A measles epidemic, introduced by Fijian chiefs returning from an official visit to Australia, reduced the Fijian population by half in only a century.

TRIBAL WARS

By the end of the eighteenth century, Fiji was divided into half a dozen small kingdoms. Firearms and the help of white men, especially the Swedish adventurer Charles Savage, who arrived in 1808, favored the rise of Bau as the most powerful tribe. Although Bau is a tiny island off the coast of Viti Levu, it dominated western Fiji by the 1850s. Its chief, Ratu Seru Epenisa Cakobau, led a confederation of tribes and proclaimed himself king of Fiji.

In 1858 Cakobau proposed that Fiji become a protectorate of Great Britain when Fiji came under pressure from the US government to pay an unjust $44,000 indemnity. The American consul, John Brown Williams, had accidentally set fire to his trading post in a spirited Fourth of July celebration. Because he had leased the buildings from the Fijian government, he insisted that the government pay him damages. He was backed by his government, for the United States was looking for ways to gain influence on Fiji.

In 1862, Cakobau came to realize that he could not sustain threats from the United States as well as the increasing encroachment into Fijian territory by his enemy the Tongan prince Enele Ma'afu and his people. He offered to cede the country to Great Britain in return for protection, but his offer was rejected.

The Fijian chiefs then organized themselves into their own confederation. This arrangement could not withstand the deep rivalry between Cakobau and Ma'afu, by then the ruler of eastern Fiji, and the confederation fell apart in 1867. By this time, thousands of white settlers from Australia, Europe, and the United States were snapping up land and planting cotton.

FORCED LABOR

In 1865, as the American Civil War greatly impeded the cotton trade out of the American South, other nations sought an alternative source of cotton. Hoping to cash in on the opportunity, thousands of British and Australians moved to Fiji and established plantations. However, plantations require large numbers of laborers, and the Fijian people were unwilling to do that work.

Laborers were enlisted from other South Pacific islands, but the recruiters often resorted to trickery and coercion to obtain workers. Potential laborers might be tricked into boarding a ship, for example, with the promise of gifts, and then once on board, find themselves locked up. The unsuspecting and unwilling people were taken to Fiji where they were forced to work, paid very little, and trapped in terrible living conditions.

This practice, called blackbirding, is essentially a form of slavery, but usually of a limited duration—three to five years, typically, and the workers were sometimes minimally paid. Officially, once the worker's time was up, he was supposed to be provided with free transport back to where he came from, but that didn't always happen.

Beginning in 1879, some sixty thousand people from India were brought to the plantations in Fiji through a system of indentured labor. This system—used throughout the British colonies in lieu of slavery, which by then was illegal—was a form of debt bondage, a means of working off personal debt through enforced labor. In India, the system was called Girmit, meaning "agreement"—a deceptive word since the usually illiterate people often had no idea what they were agreeing to—and the workers came to be called "Girmitiyas." Living conditions for the imported Girmitiyas were dismal and resembled slavery.

THE KINGDOM OF FIJI

The Fijian government was finally established in 1871, and Cakobau was crowned monarch of the Kingdom of Fiji. He and other Fijian chiefs attempted to set up a constitutional monarchy with taxation, courts, police, and other social systems. However, white settlers took offense at the idea of being ruled by the indigenous people, and they actively resisted. Meanwhile, deadly conflict erupted between the settlers—who wanted more land—and the traditional native people, called Kai Colo, who lived in the interior of Viti Levu.

Cakobau lacked any real power, and his government collapsed two years later. Fiji fell into economic chaos. In 1874 a second offer of cession to Great Britain was made, and this time it was accepted.

BRITISH COLONY

Fiji became a British colony on October 10, 1874. The first governor, Sir Arthur Gordon, felt responsible for the protection of the rights of the indigenous people and decreed that all communal land could not be sold. He also instituted an administration that retained the traditional tribal chief system. As the Fijian economy lay in tatters, the governor undertook the cultivation of sugarcane as a cash crop.

The Fijian people, however, were reluctant to work on the large plantations belonging to foreigners, so Gordon imported boatloads of indentured labor from India. This makeshift decision shaped Fijian history and politics thereafter.

Between 1879 and 1916, more than sixty thousand Indians arrived in Fiji. The indentured laborers signed five-year contracts. If they agreed to stay another five years, they were allowed to lease small plots of land in the second half of their stay, while still working on the plantations. Two-thirds of these workers did not return to India at the end of their contracts. Since no land was available for them to buy, many set up small businesses. Although the Indians themselves decided to remain in Fiji, they resented their lack of rights and thus felt less loyalty to the country than did the indigenous Fijians.

THE WORLD WARS

As a British colony, Fiji sent about seven hundred European residents and one hundred native islanders to fight in Europe in World War I. At the same time, a Fijian named Apolosi Ranawai started the Fiji Company, a movement aimed at stopping colonial exploitation by the whites. A commoner, Ranawai questioned the inherent powers of the chief system, which made this exploitation possible. Nevertheless, after being accused of sedition, Ranawai was exiled.

Fijian soldiers distinguished themselves during World War II in the Solomon Islands. More than eight thousand indigenous Fijians fought alongside the Allies in the Pacific. Virtually no Indians signed up because their demand for the same wages as paid to the Europeans was not met. For this reason, the Indian community was considered disloyal and unpatriotic. Fijian soldiers were so good at jungle warfare that they were never alleged "missing in action" if they could not be found. Instead, the phrase "not yet arrived" was used because it was actually likely that the missing soldiers would eventually turn up.

INDEPENDENCE

Although the right to vote was granted to white women and indigenous Fijians in 1963, the Indian community still faced discrimination. Having witnessed the successful struggle for independence in other British colonies in Asia and

In a 1970 ceremony, officials hoist the new flag of an independent Fiji.

Africa, Indians started to call for independence because they viewed the British to be the cause of their second-class status. The Fijians were less enthusiastic.

Nevertheless, Fiji attained independence on October 10, 1970, exactly ninety-six years after becoming a colony. By then, the Indian and Fijian populations were about equal in size. A number of people from other Pacific islands and from China had also put down roots in Fiji. The new Fijian constitution followed the British model of two parliamentary houses—a Senate composed of Fijian chiefs and a House of Representatives. Fiji also became a member of the British Commonwealth of Nations. Although the Indians did not get the full rights they demanded, they agreed to a system of communal voting.

The first post-independence elections were held in 1972, and Ratu Sir Kamisese Mara, a hereditary chief, became the first ethnic Fijian prime minister. His Alliance Party, composed of Fijians, Chinese, Europeans, and some Indians, stayed in power until 1987. Although Fiji was an independent nation, the sovereign was still the king or queen of England, represented in the country by a governor-general. The first Fijian governor-general, appointed in 1973, was Ratu George Cakobau, the great-grandson of the leader who had ceded the country to Britain. Fijian politics at the time of independence was still dominated by the chief-led clans.

THE 1987 COUPS

The 1987 elections were won by a coalition of Indian and Fijian parties that enjoyed strong support from the labor unions. Although nineteen of the twenty-eight coalition representatives were Indian, all cabinet positions of vital Fijian interest went to Fijians, and the new prime minister, Timoci Bavadra, was also a Fijian.

The new government immediately set about turning Fiji into a truly multiracial and democratic country, disregarding racist institutions and trimming away the power of hereditary chiefdoms. Faced with the loss of their privileges and financial benefits, the chiefs convinced the Fijian population to believe that the government was pro-Indian and would take away their land rights. Demonstrations and massive disorder marked the first month of

RABUKA

Sitiveni Ligamamada Rabuka was born September 13, 1948. He joined the army in 1968 and had attained the rank of lieutenant colonel when he launched his two coups d'état in 1987. Rabuka was a dedicated soldier who had served in various peacekeeping missions. An ambitious army officer, he felt his career was stagnating.

A devout Christian, Rabuka is also extremely nationalistic. For him, Fiji belongs to the Fijians. His view of the Indian community in Fiji is highly prejudicial; because Indians are not Christians, he figures, they cannot be trusted. A lay preacher, Rabuka believes that Christianity is the foundation of Fijian society. If Indians were to convert to Christianity, he would welcome them with open arms. Although he is not a chief himself, Rabuka strongly believes in the traditional chiefs system. He sees himself as a warrior for his chief. His job is to protect his clan and bring glory to his chief.

Many political observers have argued that Rabuka was a pawn in the grip of various factions when he staged his coups. The most accepted version is that his first coup was masterminded by the US Central Intelligence Agency (CIA). The coalition government of Bavadra had announced the banning of nuclear ships from Fiji, with special emphasis on a nuclear-free Pacific. This was not welcomed by the US government, which saw nuclear engagement in the Pacific as vital for its own defense. Before the first coup in May 1987, Rabuka held discussions with a former CIA deputy director, and that was taken as evidence of the involvement of the United States in the overthrow. Another theory pinpointed the influence of the Methodist Church, which wanted Fiji to be governed as a Christian fundamentalist state. Yet another version held that Rabuka had been used by the tribal chiefs to regain their privileges.

Rabuka was accused of instigating the 2000 coup and the attempted army mutiny in September 2000, and he was formally charged with mutiny in 2006. He was, nevertheless, found not guilty. As of 2018, he is the leader of the Social Democratic Liberal Party and occupies several other roles in the country. In May 2018, he was charged with corruption over anomalies in his financial declarations, a charge he claimed was politically motivated.

the new government. Indians were attacked in the streets, and government offices in Suva were fire-bombed.

On May 14, one month after the 1987 elections, Lieutenant Colonel Sitiveni Rabuka, a commoner, led a group of army officers into parliament and arrested the government leaders. He set up a new government consisting of old-timers from the Alliance Party and pronounced the governor-general, Ratu Sir Penaia Ganilau, head of state. Rabuka wanted new policies that would entrench Fijian domination in the constitution, and so Ratu Ganilau tried to work out a compromise to maintain civilian rule until the next elections.

Because Rabuka was not satisfied with the way things were turning out, he staged a second coup in September 1987. This time he declared Fiji a republic and proclaimed himself head of state. His new council of ministers was made up of powerful landowners and military officers. In October 1987, Fiji was expelled from the British Commonwealth. Ratu Mara, the chief who had become prime minister in 1972, came back as prime minister again in December, and Ratu Ganilau became the first Fijian president. Rabuka, the activist army officer, was named minister of home affairs.

RETURN TO CIVILIAN GOVERNMENT

After promulgating a totally discriminatory constitution in 1990 while in office as home affairs minister, Sitiveni Rabuka, who had given up his military career to concentrate on politics, was elected prime minister in the 1992 elections. To repair damages to the economy and regain international acceptance, Rabuka softened his views after becoming prime minister and promised to reexamine Fijian policies.

In 1994 the parliament was dissolved, and a new general election was called. During the campaign, President Ratu Penaia Ganilau died, and the Great Council of Chiefs elected Ratu Mara in his place. Rabuka was reappointed prime minister.

A new constitution came into effect in July 1998, guaranteeing full rights to the Indians and equal rights to all races. The document also changed the name of the country from Sovereign Democratic Republic of Fiji to Republic of the

Fiji Islands. All inhabitants are now known as Fiji Islanders, a title that was previously applied only to the indigenous population. The new constitution created a human rights commission and established an elected, seventy-one-member lower house of parliament. As a result of the new constitution, Fiji was readmitted to the British Commonwealth, and new elections were held in May 1999.

In the elections, Mahendra Chaudhry's Labor Party won an overwhelming number of seats, but in an attempt to appease Fijian nationalistic sentiments, the new Indian prime minister nominated many Fijian ministers to his cabinet. This decision was seen as another move to prevent a repetition of the tragic events of 1987.

TURMOIL IN THE NEW MILLENIUM

Sitiveni Rabuka points to a copy of the 1997 Fiji constitution during a media briefing at the time of the government hostage crisis of 2000.

In spite of the new leader's best intentions, Fijian nationalists could not be satisfied, and in May 2000 an armed group led by George Speight, a failed businessman, stormed Parliament and took the prime minister and most of his cabinet hostage. The army commander, Commodore Josaia Voreqe "Frank" Bainimarama, quickly stepped in and declared martial law. The hostage crisis ended in July 2000, with Ratu Mara and Rabuka accusing each other of masterminding the coup. Later that month, the military transferred power to an interim government headed by Laisenia Qarase, who remained as caretaker prime minister until the general elections in August 2001. Qarase's party won the election, and the former prime minister, Mahendra Chaudhry, became the leader of the opposition. Economic stability returned, but not for long.

In 2005 the government tried to introduce three controversial bills, of which the Reconciliation, Tolerance, and Unity (RTU) Bill was most strongly opposed. Under the guise of national reconciliation, this bill was intended to pardon the perpetrators of all the preceding coups, some of whom, at that time, were members of the government. The RTU Bill stirred up a heated friction between the government and the army, which ignited after the elections of 2006 when Bainimarama called for the resignation of the Qarase government if it failed to withdraw all controversial legislation.

On December 5, 2006, Fiji endured its fourth coup in two decades when the army chief announced on national television that the Fijian military was taking control of the country. The takeover was swift and largely peaceful, with little disruption to daily life except for some roadblocks. Foreign governments, especially Australia and New Zealand, immediately condemned the coup, and Fiji was again suspended from the Commonwealth. Financial aid from the West, especially the United States and the European Union (EU), was also withheld.

In 2007 Frank Bainimarama was appointed interim prime minister by President Ratu Josefa Iloilo, a designation that was criticized by various sectors

People wait to have lost election cards replaced at the election office in Suva.

in Fiji. The interim government then started negotiations with the EU and other donor countries for the resumption of aid to Fiji. This culminated in an undertaking by Bainimarama to hold democratic elections by March 2009. In his 2009 New Year message, however, the interim prime minister announced that elections would be held only after reforms had been made to the electoral process. Later that year, he conceded that the elections would not be held in 2009, but definitely "by September 2014." Meanwhile, yet another new constitution was signed into law in 2013, and that version remains current.

The promised elections did, in fact, take place in 2014 and were won by Bainimarama's FijiFirst Party, bringing to an end Fiji's transitional period, which had begun with his coup eight years before. Bainimarama resigned as head of the military in March 2014, and, after the elections, was sworn in as prime minister as a civilian.

In 2018, he was re-elected with just 50.02 percent of the vote. His party, FijiFirst, lost five seats in parliament but nevertheless maintained a majority. The elections also brought an increase of female representation, with ten women elected to parliament, bringing the percentage of women up to 20 percent.

INTERNET LINKS

https://www.britannica.com/place/Fiji-republic-Pacific-Ocean/History
This online encyclopedia provides a good overview of Fiji's history, with links to related stories.

http://himalmag.com/girmit-fiji
This article looks at the system of indentured servitude of Indians in Fiji.

https://www.smithsonianmag.com/travel/sleeping-with-cannibals-128958913
Although this article is mainly about cannibals in Papua New Guinea, it sheds light on the practice in South Pacific cultures.

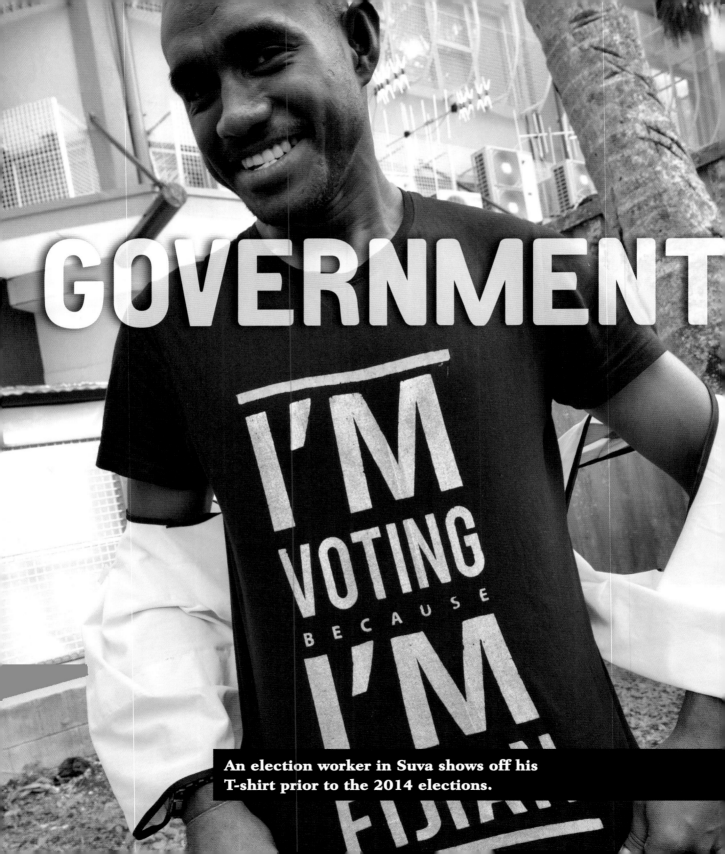

GOVERNMENT

An election worker in Suva shows off his T-shirt prior to the 2014 elections.

3

AFTER ACHIEVING INDEPENDENCE IN 1970, Fiji became a parliamentary democracy and a member of the Commonwealth. (The Commonwealth is a voluntary association of fifty-three former British colonies that are now independent and equal sovereign states. The British monarch serves as the head of the Commonwealth, but it is a purely symbolic position.) Since that time, the Fijian government has experienced several military-led coups d'etat.

Fiji is now a parliamentary republic with multiple political parties and three branches of government. The executive branch is made up of a president, a prime minister, and a cabinet of ministers. The legislature is made up of one house of parliament, and the judicial system is independent of the other branches. The country's constitution has been rewritten three times, for a total of four separate constitutions.

Although Fiji was expelled from the Commonwealth following the military coups, most recently in 2006, it was fully reinstated in 2014 after free elections were held and the military gave up command of the government.

The flag of Fiji has remained essentially the same since the colonial period. It features a British Union Jack (the national flag of the United Kingdom) in the upper left corner. In 2013, Prime Minister Frank Bainimarama announced the flag would be changed to rid it of colonial symbols. However, in 2016, those plans were abandoned for various reasons, and the flag remains the same.

The UK's Prince Charles (*right*) meets with local chiefs in Levuka, on the island of Ovalau, on the occasion of Fiji's independence in 1970.

THE CONSTITUTION

The fourth, and newest, version of the Fijian constitution was signed into law in 2013. Unlike the previous constitutions, this one provides for equal status for iTaukei (native) and Indian (Indo-) Fijians. As such, it was the first to eliminate race-based electoral rolls, race-based seat quotas, district-based representation, the unelected upper chamber, and the role of the hereditary Council of Chiefs.

The first constitution took effect in 1970, with Fiji's independence. That one provided for political dominance by the native Fijians, who at that time made up a minority of the total population, with Indo-Fijians holding a slight majority. When, despite those constitutional safeguards, a multiethnic coalition

THE PREAMBLE TO THE 2013 FIJIAN CONSTITUTION

A Constitutional preamble, or introduction, states a government's principles and purposes. The preamble establishes the source of the government's authority and sets the tone of its ideals.

WE, THE PEOPLE OF FIJI,

RECOGNISING the indigenous people or the iTaukei, their ownership of iTaukei lands, their unique culture, customs, traditions and language;

RECOGNISING the indigenous people or the Rotuman from the island of Rotuma, their ownership of Rotuman lands, their unique culture, customs, traditions and language;

RECOGNISING the descendants of the indentured labourers from British India and the Pacific Islands, their culture, customs, traditions and language; and

RECOGNISING the descendants of the settlers and immigrants to Fiji, their culture, customs, traditions and language,

DECLARE that we are all Fijians united by common and equal citizenry;

RECOGNISE the Constitution as the supreme law of our country that provides the framework for the conduct of Government and all Fijians;

COMMIT ourselves to the recognition and protection of human rights, and respect for human dignity;

DECLARE our commitment to justice, national sovereignty and security, social and economic wellbeing, and safeguarding our environment,

HEREBY ESTABLISH THIS CONSTITUTION FOR THE REPUBLIC OF FIJI.

largely made up of Indo-Fijians won in the 1987 general elections, a series of native-led coups quickly followed.

The second constitution, issued in 1990, barred non-native Fijians from access to the highest offices in the land. It also gave more power to the traditional Fijian chiefs. At that point, thousands of Indo-Fijians left the country, returning mostly to their ancestral homeland. This wave of emigration shifted the population such that the indigenous Fijians became the majority.

On the heels of international disapproval and in a bid for wider acceptance in the South Pacific, the Fijian government enacted a new constitution in 1997 that lifted racial barriers to political participation. This new constitution,

Fijian president Jioji Konrote prepares to meet Pope Francis in Vatican City in 2017.

which ensured representation of all racial groups in the government, came into effect July 27, 1998. The first elections under this more inclusive constitution took place in May 1999, and the country elected its first Indo-Fijian prime minister, Mahendra Chaudhry.

However, once again, angry native Fijians resisted, and another overthrow of the government took place in May 2000 under the leadership of native Fijian George Speight. The country was governed by military rule, which repealed the constitution and dismissed the courts. It installed Frank Bainimarama as interim prime minister.

Under this interim government, a new constitution was written and signed into law. Although the 2014 elections ended military rule and legitimized the leadership of Bainimarama as prime minister, the 2013 constitution remains in force. Its historic recognition of all Fiji's citizens as "Fijians," regardless of ethnicity, has not been fully embraced by the iTaukei, many of whom feel their ancestral claim to their own country has been undermined. In light of that, it remains to be seen whether this constitution will stand the test of time.

THE EXECUTIVE BRANCH

THE PRESIDENT is the head of state. He or she is nominated by the prime minister and elected by parliament for a three-year term and eligible for a second term. In a parliamentary democracy such as Fiji, the position of president is mainly ceremonial. In 2018, Jioji Konousi Konrote was reelected president. The next election will be in 2021.

THE PRIME MINISTER is the head of government and leader of his or her political party. The prime minister selects and presides over a cabinet of ministers, and holds the actual executive power. In the November 2018 general election, the FijiFirst party of Prime Minister Bainimarama was re-elected for another term. The next elections will take place in 2022.

THE PARLIAMENT

Under the constitution of 2013, the Fijian parliament is a unicameral, or one-house, legislature. This is a change from the past, when it consisted of two houses—the Senate, or upper house, and the House of Representatives, or lower house. Since 2014, the parliament had included fifty seats, but in 2018, one more was added. So, at this writing, the parliament consists of fifty-one members who are directly elected in a national election to serve four-year terms. The most recent elections were held in 2018, with the next to be in 2022.

On September 30, 2018, when Prime Minister Bainimarama announced the date of the upcoming elections on November 14, 2018, President Konrote dissolved parliament as is required in section 58(3) of the constitution, to await the new results.

THE GREAT COUNCIL OF CHIEFS

The Great Council of Chiefs (GCC) was a branch of the Fijian government from 1876 to 2012. In a strictly hereditary society like Fiji, the chiefs never lost their authority, despite nearly a century of British rule and four decades of independence. When Fiji changed to a Western-style government, the hereditary chiefs still wielded profound influence and power over the destiny of the country. Most of the high offices in the Fijian government and judiciary have been held by chiefs from the indigenous clans. The Fijian governors-general and presidents have almost all been hereditary chiefs. The title "Ratu" is one of the titles conferred on traditional chiefs.

Consisting of fifteen members, the Great Council of Chiefs was made up of nominated chiefs from the provincial councils as well as the prime minister, president, vice president, and the minister for Fijian affairs, who were automatic members. In addition to appointing the president of the republic and advising the president on other governmental appointments, the council also had authority over any legislation relating to land ownership and common rights. The council also chose almost half of the members of the Senate.

In 2007, during the time of the interim government that came to power following the military coup of 2006, the acting prime minister, Frank Bainimarama, suspended the Great Council of Chiefs. In 2012, the body was officially dismantled. Bainimarama said that the council was an outdated part of the country's colonial past, and that it perpetuated elitism and encouraged divisive politics.

THE JUDICIARY

The judiciary is an independent branch of the Fijian government. It consists of a system of courts, including the High Court, the Court of Appeal, and the Supreme Court. The powerful Supreme Court has the last word in any legal controversy.

The High Court includes the chief justice and up to eighteen subordinate judges. It hears civil and criminal cases, with unlimited jurisdiction. The Court of Appeal consists of the court president, who must be a judge, and a number of other judges, who may be High Court judges. The Court of Appeal hears all appeals from judgments made by the High Court. The Supreme Court is made up of the chief justice, the members of the Court of Appeal, and other appointed judges.

The chief justice is appointed by the president on the advice of the prime minister after consultation with the leader of the opposition. Other judges are appointed by the president on the recommendation of the Judicial Services Commission. All judges, including the chief justice, must step down when they reach the age of seventy.

Since 2014, the Government Buildings in Suva have housed the parliament, which had previously occupied a complex in the Veiuto section of Suva.

REGIONAL GOVERNMENT

The Fijian archipelago is divided into four administrative divisions: Northern (includes Vanua Levu, Taveuni, Rabi, and other islands to the north of the Koro Sea), Eastern (the Lau Group, Lomaiviti Group, Kadavu, Ovalau, and other islands in the Koro Sea), Central (the southeastern part of Viti Levu), and Western (the rest of Viti Levu, the Yasawa Group, and other islands to the west of Viti Levu). Each division is headed by a commissioner, who is assisted by a number of district officers.

The four divisions are further divided into fourteen provinces. The provinces are administered by a council headed by a high chief. Provinces are broken up into districts, which consist of a number of villages. The village head is a chief appointed by the village elders.

The island of Rabi, with a population of Banabans, a Micronesian people, is governed by an island council elected every four years. The Polynesian island of Rotuma, officially a dependency, is also self-administered. Its council is headed by a district officer, seven chiefs, and seven elected village representatives, as well as the most senior medical officer and the most senior agricultural officer.

NATIONAL DEFENSE

The Republic of Fiji Military Forces (RFMF) is responsible for the defense of the whole archipelago and the surveillance of the country's territorial waters. The RFMF has about 3,500 active soldiers and 6,000 reservists, which makes it one of the smallest militaries in the world. The RFMF regularly deploys contingents to United Nations (UN) peacekeeping missions worldwide, and Fijian soldiers sometimes have the opportunity to train with officers from Australia, New Zealand, and Great Britain through several agreements among the countries. Fijian soldiers are excellent at jungle warfare. They served brilliantly with Allied forces in World War II.

The 300-member RFMF Naval Squadron, formed in 1975, maintains Fiji's sovereignty at sea. The archipelago has declared a 200-mile (320-km) exclusive economic zone, and it is the responsibility of the Naval Squadron to conduct search-and-rescue operations in the area, and to ensure that no foreign ships are exploiting the marine or other resources in Fiji's exclusive economic zone.

LAND RIGHTS

There are three types of land titles in Fiji.
- Freehold property can be bought and sold freely in most areas of Fiji. Only about 8 percent of all land in Fiji is freehold.
- State lease is owned by the government and can only be leased or registered with the consent of the director of lands.
- Native or iTaukei land, which makes up some 82—87 percent of the country, can be leased but never owned by individuals. The land is owned in common by iTaukei landowning groups, or clans, called *mataqalis*. Leases are usually for a period of ninety-nine years and are monitored by the iTaukei Land Trust Board (TLTB) which grants the right to occupy land for a period of time. The TLTB is responsible for protecting the rights and interests of native owners by reserving ample land for their needs and by providing suitable land for resettlement.

NATIONAL SYMBOLS

The background color of the Fijian flag is sky blue. In the top left corner stands the Union Jack, the flag of Great Britain, to denote the relationship between Fiji and its former colonial ruler. To the center right of the flag is a shield. Across the top of the shield is a yellow lion holding a cocoa pod in its forepaws. The lion represents Great Britain and the cocoa pod heralds the natural resources of Fiji. The shield itself is separated into four sections by the Cross of Saint George, the patron saint of England. Other symbols of Fijian agriculture in three sections of the crest are the three stalks of sugarcane, a coconut palm, and a bunch of bananas. In the bottom-left section is a dove of peace, the main feature of the Fijian flag before the country was ceded to Great Britain.

The Fijian coat of arms consists of two Fijian warriors holding on to the shield that appears on the flag. A stylized canoe stands above the shield, and below it is the motto of the Fijian people—*Revreaka na Kalou ka doka na Tui*. It means, "Fear God and Honor the Queen."

The Fijian coat of arms includes important symbols on the shield: sugarcane, a coconut palm, a bunch of bananas, and a dove holding an olive branch (for peace). The golden lion at the top holds a cocoa pod.

INTERNET LINKS

https://www.britannica.com/biography/Frank-Bainimarama
This online encyclopedia provides and up-to-date profile of Frank Bainimarama.

http://www.fiji.gov.fj
This is the official portal of the Fijian government.

https://freedomhouse.org/report/freedom-world/2018/fiji
This organization rates countries on their political rights and civil liberties.

http://www.paclii.org/fj/Fiji-Constitution-English-2013.pdf
This is the 2013 Fijian constitution in PDF format.

http://thecommonwealth.org/our-member-countries/fiji/constitution-politics
The site of the Commonwealth profiles the Fijian constitution and politics.

ECONOMY

Harvested sugarcanes are piled neatly
on a plantation in Viti Levu.

4

W ITH ITS GREAT NATURAL resources, Fiji has one of the most developed economies of the Pacific Island nations. Rich in forest, mineral, and fish resources, Fiji also boasts a warm climate that supports the growing of sugarcane, tropical fruits and vegetables, cocoa, corn, rice, and other crops. On its more than three hundred tropical islands, Fiji has a multitude of beautiful white sand beaches, lush jungles, and picturesque mountains that attract thousands of tourists each year.

AGRICULTURE

Agriculture in Fiji is a mix of commercial and subsistence farming. It is still one of the driving forces of the Fijian economy, although it has been overtaken by tourism and remittances from Fijians working abroad as the main suppliers of income from overseas sources. From a labor perspective, however, agriculture remains the largest sector of the economy, employing about 44.2 percent of the total workforce in 2017. However, the sector contributed only 10.6 percent of the GDP.

Gross domestic product (GDP) is a measure of a country's total production. The number reflects the total value of goods and services produced over one year. Economists use it to determine whether a country's economy is growing or contracting. Growth is good, while a falling GDP means trouble. Dividing the GDP by the number of people in the country determines the GDP per capita (per person). This number provides an indication of a country's average standard of living—the higher the better.

In 2017, the GDP per capita in Fiji was approximately $9,800. That amount is fairly low, ranking 143rd out of 229 countries listed by the CIA World Factbook. (For comparison, the GDP per capita in the United States that year ranked number 19, at $59,500.)

SUGARCANE Sugar production was once the backbone of the Fijian economy, but the industry is in decline. The government has taken steps to diversify the country's agricultural production, and coconuts, bananas and other fruits, and cereals have become important exports.

Sugarcane cultivation is labor intensive, but has relatively low profit margins because of inefficient production methods. The crop is planted by about 22,500 farmers on small plots—typically about 10—12 acres (4—5 hectares) in size—on the northeastern sides of the islands. Many of the farmers rent the land for a period of thirty years from the government or from Fijian mataqalis, clan groups. Although most sugarcane planters are Indians, the Fijian presence is growing in the sector. After they have harvested the cane, farmers sell their crops to the Fiji Sugar Corporation (FSC), which is a government-owned enterprise. A contract between the cultivators and the FSC sets the prices of the sugarcane and also assigns a quota for each farm. The FSC runs the mills that process the canes into sugar. There are three mills in Viti Levu and one in Vanua Levu. The sugar is exported via bulk sugar terminals situated at Lautoka (Viti Levu) and Malau (Vanua Levu).

By-products of sugar include molasses, a thick dark syrup that remains after the sugar has solidified into crystals, from which rum and other liquors are made. It is also used in cooking and as cattle feed. Most of Fiji's sugar production is exported to Australia, New Zealand, Great Britain, and the European Union (EU) through a number of trade conventions.

COCONUTS Coconuts are also a major cash crop in Fiji. In 2016, Fiji was the twenty-second-largest producer of coconuts worldwide, with an output of about 41 million coconuts per year. Of that, some 35 percent was used for domestic household consumption in Fiji and another 35 percent went toward the production of copra. This is the dried meat of the coconut, from which coconut oil is manufactured. Rising international demand for coconut oil and related products has driven up the price of copra, making it a very lucrative business as well. The Fijian government is working to plant more coconut palms to take advantage of the market.

A woman carves fresh coconuts at a marketplace in Suva.

OTHER AGRICULTURAL PRODUCTS Fiji also grows and exports bananas, pineapples, watermelons, cereal, rice, corn, ginger, cocoa, and tobacco. Whereas sugarcane is planted mostly on the drier western sides of Viti Levu and Vanua Levu, the wetter areas of the islands support the growing of coconuts, ginger, cassava, taro, kava, bananas, and breadfruit. Those regions are also used for raising poultry, pigs, and cattle. In regions with intermediate rainfall, growers concentrate on vegetables, cocoa, passion fruit, and maize, as well as some sorghum, potatoes, and turmeric.

About one-sixth of the total land area of Fiji is consigned to logging businesses, and the Ministry of Forestry has started a program of reforestation to supply the timber industry. Trees grown for the lumber industry are mainly mahogany and pine. Timber exports consist mainly of sawn logs, wood chips, plywood, and veneers. There is a ban, however, on the export of logs from indigenous trees.

Accommodations like these attract tourists to enjoy Fiji's tropical splendors.

TOURISM

The strongest performer in the Fijian economy, tourism directly accounts for more than 17 percent of GDP, and indirectly about 44 percent. It is the largest money-earner, employing an estimated 42,500 people in 2016.

Fiji is by far the most popular tourist destination in the South Pacific, attracting 842,884 visitors in 2017. Most tourists come from New Zealand, the United States, Australia, and Asia. Since the start of regular nonstop flights from Los Angeles in the mid-1990s, the number of American tourists to Fiji has increased steadily. Americans now make up about 10 percent of all arrivals.

Most tourists stay in large beach resorts on the west coast of Viti Levu. They are attracted by the warm weather, excellent diving, and duty-free shopping. The majority of hotels are owned by foreigners and managed by European hoteliers. Front-line jobs, such as tour guides and hotel clerks and managers, go to Fijians, while Indians fill the technical positions. The Fijian Visitors Bureau (FVB) is responsible for promoting tourism to the country, using media and goodwill activities.

MINING

Fiji is located on what is called the "Pacific Ring of Fire," so called for its earthquake and volcanic activity. However, mining companies know that gold is associated with this region as well.

The only mineral that is exploited in Fiji on an industrial scale is gold. A small amount of silver is also produced. The country's primary gold mine is at Vatukoula in northern Viti Levu, where miners have been extracting gold since 1935. Production has increased in recent years with the updating of mining equipment.

Extensive copper and gold deposits have been found at Namosi, to the northwest of Suva, on Viti Levu. In January 2008, the Namosi Joint Venture (NJV), owned by Australian and Japanese investors, began to explore the area, and these investigations revealed that the metal was in fact of a higher grade than previously thought. With the elevated prices of metals on the world markets, the Fijian government is eager to get the project underway. The company has been granted an exploratory license through 2020.

Namosi is targeted to become one of the largest mines in the world, and local people worry that it will catastrophically alter the landscape of Viti Levu and have a wide-ranging impact on the lifestyle and environment of the local population.

FISHING

Being an island nation, Fiji naturally depends a great deal on fishing for both food and trade. In the early twenty-first century, fish products accounted for nearly 10 percent of export revenue, with canned fish being the country's fourth-largest export. Most of the exported canned fish is tuna, but mackerel is also canned for the local market. The largest market for Fiji's canned tuna is the EU, while a large amount of refrigerated or iced yellowfin tuna is sent to the United States and Japan to be consumed as sashimi (raw fish). Other export products are trochus shell, shark's fins, and bêche-de-mer—sea cucumber.

Fiji's fisheries sector has been struggling, however. From 2007 to 2014, production of fish from coastal fisheries in Fiji decreased at a rate of 6 percent.

This was largely due to overfishing, which has depleted the fish populations in the region. According to the Fiji Tuna Boat Owners Association, approximately 75 percent of the domestic fishing fleet ceased operation in the last five to ten years.

By 2014, Fiji's tuna industry was on the verge of collapse because most of its fleets were not able to catch enough fish. Whereas in 2010—2011, the average catch was about two hundred albacore tuna a day, by 2014 it had fallen to about fifteen to twenty fish a day. That year, the value of fisheries and aquaculture production in Fiji was estimated at $250.9 million, and the sector made up 1.83 percent of Fiji's gross domestic product

The increased incursion of huge fishing vessels from other countries—particularly China, but also the United States, Japan, South Korea, and Europe—into Fiji's waters hasn't helped. Fiji plans to cut back on the number of licenses it issues to these vessels, but some neighboring Pacific islands continue to sell unlimited numbers of licenses, which only encourages tremendous overfishing. Even if the vessels stay outside of Fiji's borders at sea, they fish heavily in

Customers consider the fresh fish for sale at the Nadi fish market on Viti Levu.

Water plays a major part in the Fijian economy, which makes sense for the island nation. However, the water in this case is fresh, not seawater. Fiji Water is a brand-name, premium, still (nonsparkling) bottled water derived from Fiji and shipped to more than sixty countries overseas, including the United States. In dollar value, it is Fiji's top export.

Fiji Water is pumped from an underground aquifer deep beneath the Nakauvadra Range where it is protected by layers of soft rock and clay. The company claims its water not only is pure but also has a "unique mineral profile," with high levels of calcium, magnesium, and silica.

In 1996, a Canadian businessman began bottling pure artesian water from a multimillion-dollar plant at Yaqara in northern Viti Levu. The next year, the company started exporting its square bottles to the United States, where it is now a well-recognized product. In 2004, the company was sold to a private US corporation now called The Wonderful Company, and is now headquartered in Los Angeles.

Fiji Water is now Fiji's number-one export item, having surpassed fish, gold, and sugar. In 2016, it accounted for 13.5 percent of all exports from Fiji.

In 2010, the company and the Fijian government became embroiled in a well-publicized conflict when the government significantly raised the company's taxes. The company balked, shut down operations, and threatened to leave Fiji. Such a move would have left hundreds of its Fijian employees out of work. However, in the resulting standoff, the company backed down after the government threatened to give the aquifer to another company. Production resumed and the company paid the required taxes.

Ironically, despite the company's claim to be "green," environmentalists strongly disagree. The very concept of bottled water—shipping water thousands of miles to locations that already have an abundance of perfectly clean water—is one that is seen as enormously destructive. Taking into consideration the fossil fuels used in the manufacture of the bottles and the transportation of the bottled water to its major markets, as well as the carbon emissions during both processes, environmentalists believe they have a reasonable concern about the industry.

regions just beyond the borders, intercepting migrating schools of fish before they can enter Fiji's waters. Illegal vessels—of which there are many—only compound the problem.

In 2018, Fiji signed on to a UN treaty called the Port State Measures Agreement (PSMA), the first binding international agreement to specifically target illegal, unreported, and unregulated fishing. Implementing the measures will help Fiji to identify vessels of interest and illegal vessels that may visit its ports.

In addition to these ongoing problems, when Tropical Cyclone Winston hit Fiji during February and March 2016, it caused $2.9 million worth of damages to the already strained fisheries sector.

TRANSPORTATION

Infrastructure is adequate in the larger islands. There are about 2,140 miles (3,440 km) of roads, of which 1,048 miles (1,686 km) are paved. Public transportation, such as the bus service, reaches most districts of the major islands, and taxis are readily available in the urban centers. Fares are fixed

Buses are filled with travelers at the busy terminal in Suva's city center.

by the government. Many Fijians travel by "running cabs." They are shared taxis, and the fares depend on the number of passengers. Another cheap method of transportation is the truck. Passengers ride in the back of a small, hooded truck for a sometimes bumpy shared trip. Most roads in Fiji are narrow, crooked, and poorly maintained. What is more, drivers have to contend with potholes, landslides, and stray animals (dogs, cows, and horses), all of which can be especially dangerous at night.

The Fijian international airport is at Nadi. An airport at Nausori handles regional and domestic interisland flights. The national carrier is Fiji Airways, which flies to various remote destinations in the Pacific Ocean as well as Australia, New Zealand, Japan, and the United States. Domestic services are provided by Fiji Link (the domestic arm of Fiji Airways) and Pacific Island Air and Turtle Airways, which operate seaplanes that take off and land on water. Aside from the air services, interisland travel is supplied by a number of ferries and smaller craft.

INTERNET LINKS

https://atlas.media.mit.edu/en/profile/country/fji
This interactive graphic provides a visual representation of Fiji's export and import statistics.

http://www.fsc.com.fj/keyfacts.html
The Fiji Sugar Corporation provides an overview of the history of sugarcane in Fiji.

https://onlinelibrary.wiley.com/doi/full/10.1111/apv.12144
This scholarly article from 2017 takes an in-depth look at the political, socioeconomic, and environmental impact of Fiji Water in Fiji.

https://www.worldfishing.net/news101/regional-focus/fiji-battling -to-save-it-waters
This article takes a good look at the challenges facing Fiji's fisheries.

ENVIRONMENT

Old world fruit bats, one of many bat species called flying foxes, hang in a tree on Viti Levu, Fiji.

5

F FIJI IS A PARADISE, IT IS A POLLUTED one. Although the environmental degradation is not as serious in Fiji as in many other developing countries, countless practices, by both the local population and commercial enterprises, are a cause for concern. The major environmental issues today are deforestation, soil erosion, and pollution.

Since independence, more than 30 percent of forests have been wiped out by commercial interests. Soil erosion is brought about by inadequate agricultural methods and a change in rainfall patterns. But most serious of all is land and marine pollution. Rivers and the sea are polluted by pesticides and chemicals used in the sugar and fishing industries as well as by the mindless dumping of domestic waste into the island waterways.

THE NATURAL ENVIRONMENT

Fiji's forests cover an area of 2.3 million acres (931,000 hectares) out of a total land mass of 4.5 million acres (1.82 million ha), most of them standing on communally owned native land. More than 40 percent of the forest cover remains intact, and some islands, such as Taveuni, still have contiguous forest stretching from the high-altitude cloud forest all the way down to the sea. The largest tract of virgin primary forest is the Sovi Basin on Viti Levu, which has become an important area for sustaining birdlife.

The critically endangered Fijian flying fox, or monkey-faced bat, lives only in the cloud forest of Taveuni Island. Only six individuals of this species have ever been seen! The population size is estimated at fewer than one thousand due to habitat loss—much of Fiji's cloud forests have been converted to mahogany plantations. Climate change is anticipated to shrink cloud forests worldwide, resulting in further habitat loss.

A waterfall in a park in Suva creates a serene scene of tropical beauty.

Three types of forest exist in Fiji—the tropical rain forest, the mangrove forest, and the dry forest growing on the leeward (protected from the wind) sides of the islands. Once covered with sandalwood, casuarinas, ironwood, and bamboo, the dry forest is steadily receding as the land is cleared for agriculture, such as sugarcane or pine plantations.

The rain forest is the habitat of some 1,600 species of plants, 56 percent of which are endemic. Local hardwoods such as kauvula and kandamu, as well as the softer Fijian kauri, which is very common in furniture making, encompass the bulk of rain forest trees. The banyan tree is another beautiful, majestic feature of the forest. On the forest floor, elegant orchids and ferns grow extravagantly, while vines climb up to the canopy.

Fiji's rain forest animal life is rather sparse in variety of mammals. The bulk of land-based species consists of reptiles and amphibians. Of note are Fiji's endemic frogs, which are terrestrial breeders, undergoing direct development. That is, tiny froglets, or miniature frogs—rather than tadpoles—emerge from hatched eggs. Insects are more plentiful, with at least forty-four varieties of butterflies. Birdlife is much more impressive, with twenty-seven endemic species of land-based birds. These make up 46 percent of all land birds in the country. Flashy parrots, sleek pigeons, and long-tailed fantails create vivid patches of color in the forest.

The mangrove forest provides an important breeding ground for many of the reef fishes. Some 44,500 acres (18,000 ha) of mangrove buffer much of the coastline along Viti Levu and Vanua Levu, protecting the shore from the impact of hurricanes and wave erosion. Here, among the thick root tentacles, mangrove herons, kingfishers, lorries, and orange-breasted honeyeaters abound, as well as shrimp, small fish, and mud crabs.

MARINE LIFE

The most distinctive aspect of underwater Fiji is the 3,900 square miles (10,100 sq km) of coral that twist and turn around every island. Fiji's many species of corals make up 42 percent of the world's coral species. Providing a natural habitat for thousands of species of plants, fish, and other animals, these amazing structures are comparable to the rain forests in terms of biodiversity. More than three hundred species of coral live in Fijian waters, both hard and soft varieties. Soft coral thrives in clear water less than 50 yards (46 m) deep, with an ideal temperature between 75 and 85 degrees Fahrenheit (24°C and 29°C). Thus, the slightest imbalance causes the reef to die, leading to dire consequences for the varieties of wildlife that make their homes among the corals. Global warming due to climate change is causing exactly that imbalance, and scientists warn that the world's corals could all be gone by the end of the century.

The most colorful coral inhabitants are the reef fishes that make underwater Fiji look like a giant tropical aquarium. More than one thousand species have been identified, with clown anemonefish, or clownfish, being most prolific. Equally ubiquitous is the damselfish, which comes in a variety of colors. Larger species, including grouper and barracuda, are less colorful. Of the three types of rays present in Fiji waters, the manta ray likes to bury itself in the sandy

A young woman swims underwater over a coral reef at a resort on Vanua Levu.

SAVE THE TURTLES!

*Of the world's seven species of sea turtles, four are common to the waters of Fiji, and all four of them are in trouble. According to the International Union for Conservation of Nature (IUCN) Red List of Threatened Species, the hawksbill (*Eretmochelys imbricate*) and Pacific leatherback (*Dermochelys coriacea*) turtles are critically endangered, while the loggerhead (*Caretta caretta*) and green (*Chelonia mydas*) turtles are listed as endangered.*

Illegal and excessive hunting are the primary reasons the populations of these turtles are in decline, but climate change is also having an effect. For one thing, beach erosion from rising sea levels destroys nesting sites. As it is, the sea turtles face a daunting series of hazards. Mother Nature herself already poses a challenge to turtle reproduction. On average, turtles lay one hundred eggs in each nest. Of those, about ninety will hatch, but only one of the original one hundred will grow to adulthood. Human activity only diminishes those odds, even when it's unintended. Tuna fishing fleets using longline and  *purse seine methods often inadvertently catch turtles on their hooks or in their nets.*

Despite a national ban on turtle hunting, put in place in 2009, the practice continues. Turtle meat is a choice delicacy for Fijians and is also an essential ingredient in some ceremonial feasting. Enforcement of the ban is rather lax, and penalties are low, so ecologists are trying to use education as a means of changing attitudes. Many citizens are cooperating with conservation efforts and have willingly given up this favorite food for the good of the turtles.

bottom of a lagoon. The rarest is the beautiful spotted eagle ray, which prefers to hunt in the open ocean.

Outside the reef, dolphins, sharks, and whales patrol the seas, sometimes coming into a lagoon to hunt. Two types of dolphin swim year-round in Fijian waters: spinner and bottlenose. They live in groups called pods, mainly around the Lomaiviti Islands. As for sharks, a dozen species are found in Fiji, the most common being the small reef sharks (blacktips and whitetips). Big sharks, such as hammerhead and tiger, prefer to remain along the outer edges of reefs. The aggressive bull shark, on the other hand, likes to lurk in the murky coastal waters and mangrove estuaries. Pilot whales can be seen quite frequently, while humpback whales migrate to the islands from June to October.

ENDANGERED SPECIES

As of 2001, the International Union for Conservation of Nature (IUCN) had listed four species of mammal, nine types of birds, six species of reptiles and one type of amphibian as being endangered in Fiji, as well as sixty-four species of plants.

Many reptiles are among the most endangered animals in Fiji. Critically imperiled, the Fiji crested iguana faces habitat destruction from logging activities as well as predation from introduced species such as the mongoose and feral cats. Nevertheless, conservation efforts are underway, with the National Trust of Fiji playing a principal role.

Three species of bats are on the endangered list. The most vulnerable to extinction is the Fijian flying fox, or monkey-faced bat. Because its habitat is restricted to the mountain cloud forest of Taveuni, it is one of the world's rarest creatures and Fiji's only endemic mammal. The other two are the Fiji blossom bat, the world's only long-tailed cave dwelling fruit bat, which is found only in Fiji and Vanuatu, and the Pacific sheath-tailed bat.

The Fiji petrel is on the critically endangered list, and it rarely has been sighted since its discovery in 1855. It is unique to the island of Gau and after 1984 was thought to be extinct. Its first-ever photograph was taken in May

A critically endangered Fiji crested iguana stands on a log on Viti Levu.

A humphead wrasse, also called a Napoleon fish, swims along a coral reef.

2009 by an expedition organized by NatureFiji—MareqetiViti, and a recovery plan is currently under way with the communities on Gau. Another very rare bird is the red-throated lorikeet, which has not been sighted since 1993. It is feared to be extinct.

Among fish species, the humphead wrasse is fast declining in numbers due to overfishing and its own natural slow growth. Although it is a protected species, the wrasse is popular in restaurants and during feasts. To catch the large wrasses, some unscrupulous fishermen have been known to squirt highly toxic sodium cyanide on them, threatening the life of the whole reef ecosystem. Several freshwater fish are also considered vulnerable, but as yet there is no legislation to protect them. The rarest of them all is the redigobius, a small, recently discovered goby, which is so rare that it does not even have a common name.

NATURE RESERVES

The Fijian government has established six national parks, four of them on Viti Levu, as protected areas of outstanding natural beauty. Administered by the National Trust of Fiji, most of the parks are located in the interior and encompass large areas of rain forest. The exception is the Sigatoka Sand Dunes, Fiji's first national park and the most extensive dune complex in the Pacific. Spread over 1,600 acres (650 ha) of southwestern Viti Levu, the parabolic—bowl-shaped—dunes were formed over millions of years through coastal erosion. In places, they can rise to a height of 260 feet (79 m). Half of the dunes, however, are unstable. The area can be explored on official trails. It was there the elaborate Lapita pottery was first discovered, pointing to two thousand years of human settlement, and archaeological relics and human remains are still being uncovered.

Located in the steep hills above Nadi and Lautoka, Koroyanitu Park is the only national heritage park on Viti Levu. It was established to preserve

Fiji's only unlogged upland tropical montane forest and cloud forest in order to create revenue and employment for the inhabitants of the six villages found inside the park. The park is crossed by the Mount Evans range, which contains several peaks above 3,000 feet (915 m). The tallest is Mount Batilamu at 3,920 feet (1,195 m).

Within the cool vastness of the park lies the Garden of the Sleeping Giant. Housing more than two thousand varieties of orchids, this garden at one time belonged to the estate of the late Raymond Burr, an American actor. More than twenty-two bird species have been recorded in the park, including the goshawk, peregrine falcon, white-throated pigeon, barking pigeon, and masked shining parrot. The two other national parks on Viti Levu are the Nausori Highlands west of Nadi and Colo-i-Suva, just outside the capital.

The Garden of the Sleeping Giant, once owned by a Hollywood movie star, is now open to the public.

Some ecotourists take part in a kava drinking ceremony on Vorovoro Island, hosted by members of the Mali tribe.

ECOTOURISM

Since the mid-1990s, the government of Fiji has recognized the dangers of mass tourism to the environment and has made the promotion of ecotourism one of the cornerstones of its visitor policy. The Fiji Ecotourism Association was formed in 1995, defining ecotourism as "a form of nature-based tourism which involves responsible travel to relatively undeveloped areas to foster an appreciation of nature and local cultures." National policy recognizes ecotourism as one component of sustainable development involving local participation. Complementing—not competing with—conventional tourism, ecotourism brings together various stakeholders, in particular small communities that can earn a living while making sustainable use of their natural resources.

Ecotourism takes several forms in Fiji. Many resorts have adopted environmentally friendly practices, such as installing water-treatment facilities and making use of local materials. They also educate their guests about natural conservation, especially of the marine environment, and invite them to take part in turtle rescue and coral management. Another component of ecotourism is provided by the national parks, which offer hiking, river rafting, and other adventure-based activities. The cultural part is achieved through village visits and home stays, where visitors can sample village life and take part in various activities, such as the traditional *yaqona* ceremony that marks special occasions.

The first Fijian resort to become a member of the International Ecotourism Society was Matava Resort on Kadavu. At this most environmentally friendly hotel in Fiji, all waste is either recycled, composted, used in the organic garden, or fed to the local pigs. Power is generated by solar panels, and rooms do not have air-conditioning or electric fans. The buildings are made with local materials, and hot water is available only in the shower, heated by propane burners.

**https://www.aljazeera.com/news/2018/01/fiji-pm-losing-battle
-save-coral-reefs-180117164653362.html**
This article discusses the effect of climate change on Fiji's coral reefs.

**https://www.amuraworld.com/en/topics/conservancy-report/
articles/5993-fiji-coral-reefs**
Beautiful photos of Fiji's various coral reefs are featured on this site.

**https://www.lonelyplanet.com/fiji/taveuni/travel-tips-and
-articles/diving-and-snorkelling-in-fiji/40625c8c-8a11-5710-a052
-1479d2763849**
This article, with beautiful photos, focuses on snorkeling around some
of Fiji's reefs.

https://naturefiji.org
This organization works to enhance and protect Fiji's
natural environment.

https://naturefiji.org/category/endangered-species
The Nature Fiji archive of endangered animals is found on this page.

**https://www.nytimes.com/2017/11/17/climate/islands-climate
-change-un-bonn.html**
This article looks at the climate change challenges facing
island nations.

**https://www.nytimes.com/2017/01/02/world/asia/on-a-fijian
-island-hunters-become-conservators-of-endangered-turtles.html**
Fijians are learning to give up eating turtles and are instead working to
protect them.

FIJIANS

A boy swings on a rope in the Lavena
village on Taveuni Island.

6

Mahendra Chaudhry became Fiji's first Indo-Fijian prime minister in 1999. His term was short-lived, however. A coup removed him from office one year later.

ALL INHABITANTS OF THE FIJIAN archipelago are called Fiji Islanders, or Fijians. The island nation has the most multicultural population of all South Pacific countries. Native Fijians make up more than half of all inhabitants. In 2010, the country passed a law replacing the term "Fijian" with "iTaukei" when referring to the original and native settlers of Fiji. Therefore, the word Fijian now denotes nationality, not ethnicity.

The iTaukei make up about 56.8 percent of the population. The other large ethnic group is the Indian community—meaning South Asians whose roots are the country of India—which accounts for 37.5 percent of the population. The rest is composed of Rotumans, Chinese, Europeans, and other Pacific Islanders, as well as those who are of mixed heritage.

In 2017, Fiji had an estimated population of 920,938. Approximately 75 percent live on Viti Levu, in towns such as Nadi and Lautoka, and in the sugarcane-growing regions of Ba and Rewa. Vanua Levu supports 15 percent of the population, and the remaining 10 percent is scattered among more than one hundred islands. The larger towns on Viti Levu are quite cosmopolitan in the makeup of their residents, while the smaller islands and villages are composed almost entirely of native Fijians. Indians predominate in areas where sugarcane is grown.

ITAUKEI

An iTaukei man says, "Bula!" ("Hello!")

The indigenous Fijians are of Austronesian stock and share a common ancestry with various peoples in Southeast Asia and Oceania. This diverse group inhabits almost half the globe, ranging from Madagascar in the Indian Ocean to Easter Island in the Pacific Ocean. Displaying a variety of physical characteristics, the iTaukei are related to both the Melanesians to the west and the Polynesians to the east. In general, they are slightly less dark and are larger in stature than other Melanesians, especially the native Fijians living in the eastern islands. Those islanders in the interior and on the western side of Viti Levu, however, where close contact with Polynesians has been less frequent, are darker than their compatriots. Although Fiji is geographically situated in Melanesia, iTaukei society has been most heavily influenced by the Polynesian chiefly system.

The iTaukei live in villages along the rivers or on the coast. Each led by a hereditary chief, these small communities can have anywhere between fifty and four hundred residents. Indigenous villages are hard to come upon because they are always located far from the main roads. In western Viti Levu, villages are smaller still, and social behavior is less rigid. An outstanding commoner who displays great leadership qualities can be elevated to the rank of high chief.

Most iTaukei families are self-sustaining, growing their own food and making their own clothing. Although each family farms its own plot of land, communal life is very important. Fishing, village maintenance work, building new homes, and ceremonies are performed together as a group. Individuals are discouraged from rising above the community standard. iTaukei who start a business are often stifled by the demands of their relatives. It is normal for iTaukei to claim favors from those who are better off in the clan. This behavior is called *kerekere* (kay-reh-KAY-ray).

INDIANS

Most Indians in Fiji are descendants of the indentured laborers who were brought to work in the country's sugarcane fields by the British. The first Indians arrived in 1879 from the populous provinces of Bihar, Uttar Pradesh, and Bengal (today's Bangladesh). Subsequent arrivals came mainly from South India. They were dark-skinned, with straight black hair and black eyes. Although the system of indentured labor was abolished in 1919, Indians continued to migrate to Fiji until 1931. The later arrivals, mainly from northern Gujarat and Punjab, were wealthier. They came to set up trading businesses that catered to the large Indian community.

Most of the indentured laborers chose to remain in Fiji at the end of their contracts. As they were not allowed to own land, many Indians invested their savings in businesses. Most village stores are owned by Indian storekeepers, who are very active in the retail sector. They continue to dominate the professions and commerce.

Indian Fijian worshippers enter the Sri Siva Hindu temple in Nadi, Fiji. It is the largest Hindu temple in the Southern Hemisphere.

THE INDENTURE SYSTEM

When the British took control of Fiji, they resorted to Indian indentured labor to work in the sugarcane plantations they had set up. This system had worked well for them in Mauritius and Trinidad, and the governor-general had no doubt that it was the answer to a labor situation in Fiji. Negotiations with the Indian government started in 1878, and the first 450 laborers arrived in 1879. They were contracted for an initial period of five years, after which they were free to go home at their own expense. If they renewed their contracts for another five years, their return passage would be paid for them. In the first five years, the indentured laborers had to work exclusively for their employers, cutting canes for long hours a day. During the term of the second contract, they were allowed to lease small plots of land or to raise cattle.

Many Indians saw the system as a way to escape the famine and abject poverty of their home country. Others were hoodwinked into signing up. The labor agents misrepresented the distance between Fiji and India and painted a rosy picture of life on the plantations, with promises of wealth and great prospects. They also concealed the penalties for breaking their contracts. It was only when they arrived on the plantations that they discovered the reality.

The laborers had to cut canes for twelve hours a day, and sometimes even longer, with only very short breaks for meals. Food was strictly rationed, and wages were low. If the laborer failed to complete the daily quota, his pay was cut and he was physically punished. Moreover, living conditions were terrible; the workers had to put up with overcrowding and no leisure. Essentially, the system was little better than slavery.

Most of the people brought to Fiji under the indenture system were men. Only forty women were allowed into the nation for every one hundred men, though in reality even fewer women came. This gender imbalance led to the helpless women being assaulted and traded like livestock. Girls were forced into marriages and became mothers at a very young age. Adultery was rampant, and remarriage became a widespread behavior.

Despite the inhumane conditions, two-thirds of the laborers opted to stay in the country after their contracts had been fulfilled. For many of the lower-caste Indians, life in Fiji offered better prospects than in India, and many sent for their families. Between 1879 and 1916, about 2,000 Indians were transported to the archipelago each year, bringing the total to 60,537. When the system was abolished, some 40,000 Indians were living in Fiji.

Although most of them have been in Fiji for four generations, the Indo-Fijians—as Fiji-born people of Indian descent sometimes prefer to be called—have retained their ancestral beliefs and religions. Most marriages still take place within the same caste, although people from different castes interact freely in daily activities.

The Indian community is divided between Hindus (80 percent) and Muslims (15 percent), with a small fellowship of Christians. The Sikhs and Gujaratis, who did not belong to the indenture system, are considered elite. In general, Indians still associate more closely with other members of the same home province or dialect.

In 1986, Indians made up 48 percent of the population compared with 46 percent of native Fijians. The coups of 1987 provoked a mass exodus of Indians, and since then Indians have accounted for 80 percent of all emigration from Fiji. According to official data, more than one hundred thousand Indians have left the country since 1987. Many Indian intellectuals and much Indian money left Fiji for Australia and the United States. Today Indians make up less than 40 percent of the population.

ROTUMANS

Situated about 289 miles (465 km) north of Fiji, the island of Rotuma became part of Fiji when it was ceded to Great Britain following wars between different factions on the island. The British decided that it was to be administered as part of the colony of Fiji, with a resident commissioner. Today the small island is a dependency of Fiji.

Making up about 1.2 percent of the Fijian population, Rotumans form a distinct minority in the country because they long remained fairly isolated from the other groups. Although they have been associated with Fiji for more than a century, they have kept their distinctive culture and language. Rotumans do not practice social class distinctions, although there are chiefs. Social life is based on kinship relationships and communal sharing.

The Rotuman population is growing fast, increasingly made up of children and youths. The great majority of Rotumans live elsewhere in Fiji, with fewer than two thousand remaining on Rotuma itself. There, the number of working-age people is very low, and elderly residents predominate. The Rotuman community in urban centers on other islands is well educated. Most of the males are employed in skilled occupations or the professions, while an equal number of women are divided between working and homemaking.

BANABANS

Originally from Banaba (formerly Ocean Island) in Kiribati, the Banabans were resettled on Rabi Island off the coast of Vanua Levu in 1942. This shift first occurred after British phosphate mining stripped their island bare, and again when Japanese military forces invaded it during World War II. The island of Rabi was purchased with royalties paid to the Banaban population by the mining companies.

In the 1970s the Banabans sued the British government and the British Phosphate Commission for compensation. With the money they were awarded, they established various companies and even built a new house for every couple getting married on the island. Lack of business acumen, however, led to the failure of all those ventures, and today the Banaban population is as poor as when it arrived on Rabi.

The Banaban population on Rabi numbers about five thousand, most of whom work in agriculture or fishing. The Banabans at first did not take well to life in Fiji. Many died from diseases because their bodies, accustomed to the equatorial heat of Banaba, could not get used to the lower temperatures in Fiji. Originally governed by a council of leaders, Rabi today is administered from Fiji through a Rabi Island Council. The Banaban administrators have set up various training programs for women and young people so that the community may become more self-reliant.

OTHERS

The rest of the Fijian population is made up of Chinese, Europeans, and people of mixed background.

The Chinese in Fiji are descended mainly from settlers who arrived to start general stores or small businesses a century ago. Many originated in Southeast

Asia, bringing with them their traditions. Today they are still prominent in the business and retail sectors and are generally well accepted by the Fijians. Many of them are wealthy merchants who have worked hard and prospered over the years. They tend to specialize in restaurant work and commerce. Although the Chinese have retained their language, customs, and religion, many of the Chinese today have married freely with the other ethnic groups. The local Chinese population is augmented by mainland Chinese who come to Fiji to operate truck farms.

The European community is composed mainly of the descendants of Australians and New Zealanders who came to Fiji in the nineteenth century to set up or work on cotton, copra, or sugarcane plantations. Many of them married Fijian women. Generally, they are urban dwellers, and most of them are well educated and better off than native Fijians and Indians.

INTERNET LINKS

https://www.frommers.com/destinations/fiji/in-depth/the-people
This travel site provides a good look at the Fijian people.

https://minorityrights.org/country/fiji-islands
This website for the world's minority peoples includes this page discussing Fiji, with links to information about Indo-Fijians, Rotumans, and Banabans.

LIFESTYLE

A child watches a young woman cut a coconut in Lavena village on Taveuni Island.

7

FIJI HAS A MULTIETHNIC POPULATION, and to some extent, Fijians share a common culture. But in many ways, people's lifestyles depend on their ethnic and racial heritage, as well as on where they live. Fiji has a large urbanized population. More than half of the total population lives in cities, especially Suva, which is becoming very crowded. In urban areas, Fijians and Indians tend to live in different neighborhoods; in smaller towns they may live closer together. City life revolves around work or school during the week and church on weekends. Village life is more communal, with villagers getting together to share drinks or gossip in the evenings.

Nevertheless, race relations are mostly harmonious. Fijians and Indians work together amicably and freely interact socially. Some may even call one another "brother." Although a single national identity has not developed, the two races live side by side with tolerance, while retaining their ancestral customs and traditions. Perhaps the one truly national

In 2003, the descendants of the Nabutautau villagers that killed and ate the Christian missionary Thomas Baker in 1867 presented one hundred *tabuas*, or whale's teeth, to Baker's descendants in an elaborate ceremony of apology. The native Fijians came to believe the cannibalism of Baker had brought a curse upon their village, and offered the ceremony in hopes of breaking the curse.

activity is the drinking of kava, a slightly intoxicating drink made from the dried roots of the pepper plant.

BULA!

Despite their scary past reputation as cannibals and fierce warriors, the Fijian people are very friendly and courteous. *Bula* (MBU-lah) is the most common expression of greeting among Fijians. More than a simple "hello," this word means "life." It is used to welcome guests, when meeting friends, or simply as a form of communication. Even though they tend to be soft-spoken and rather reserved, Fijians greet each other with a smile and a cheerful "Bula!" or "Good morning." Except in the large towns, the same civility is extended to strangers. Fijians today enjoy a reputation for generous hospitality and warm friendliness, a stark contrast to the fear they aroused in visitors only a century ago.

These thatched-roof houses on Vanua Levu are a good example of traditional Fijian *bures*.

FIJIAN ETIQUETTE

Fijian society is highly structured, with many social norms governing interactions. For harmony between neighbors, people talk softly and go about their daily activities with measured movements. Shouting or talking loudly is rude. Even small children do not run around screaming their heads off.

Since Fijian villages are private property, all visitors, including those from towns or other villages, have to obtain the headman's permission before entering. They should be bareheaded, as only the chief is allowed to wear a hat. Many restrictions apply to a Fijian's head. It is considered the most sacred part of the body, so it is extremely disrespectful to touch a person's head. Even patting children's heads is almost taboo. In the old days, anyone touching a chief's head, even by accident, was put to death.

Another set of rules governs a person's feet. Anyone entering a traditional Fijian house, or *bure* (MBOO-reh), must remove his or her shoes and leave them at the door. The person also has to stoop in a sign of respect to the owners and the people inside.

CUSTOMS AND TRADITIONS

Fijians are very conservative and religious. They have, nonetheless, clung to many customs predating their conversion to Christianity. Some of the earlier practices, including tattooing and the circumcision of young girls and boys, have been abandoned. But many traditional communal activities are still alive. Several relate to fishing.

On Lakeba Island in the Lau Group, the villagers perform an annual shark-calling ritual in October or November. About a month before the event, the spot on the reef where the calling will take place is marked off so that no one fishes or swims near it. On the designated day, the caller stands up to his neck in the water and starts chanting, which is believed to attract sharks. Popular belief holds that during the chanting, a school of sharks, led by a white shark, is lured to the spot. The villagers then move in to kill the sharks, except for the white one. The sharks are cooked and eaten later.

Yaqona (*yang-GOH-nah*) is the Fijian word for kava, a pepper-like plant that is highly important in the culture. The roots and stems of the plant are dried and pounded into a powder. Mixing the powder with water produces a slightly narcotic beverage also called yaqona, or kava. Most outsiders find the beverage to be quite vile-tasting, but it's by far the most important drink in Fiji.

One of the most elaborate rituals in Fiji is the yaqona ceremony. It is performed with utmost gravity to mark births, marriages, deaths, official visits, or the installation of a new chief. Only traditional utensils are used—the tanoa (*TAH-nwah*) is a large wooden bowl in which the drink is mixed, and the bilo (*MBIH-loh*) is a cup made from half a coconut shell. A yaqona ceremony is full of pomp and ritual.

All participants sit in a semicircle on a large woven mat in front of the tanoa. A reddish cord decorated with cowry shells hangs from the front of the bowl and is stretched toward the guest of honor or most important chief. Stepping over the cord is not allowed. The kava mixer and the kava server stand behind the tanoa. Women do not usually take part in the ceremony. When they do, they sit behind the men and are never offered the first drink unless they are the guest of honor.

To prepare kava, the tanoa is filled with water. Then the mixer places some powdered kava in a cloth, dips the cloth in the water, and gently massages it. The water slowly turns opaque brown as the drink is mixed. When the mixer thinks it is done, he fills a bilo and passes it to the guest of honor to taste. If the latter finds it acceptable, the mixer runs his hands around the tanoa, claps three times, and proclaims, "The kava is ready, my chief."

Now the drinking proper starts. Squatting before the tanoa, the mixer fills a cup and passes it to the server, who gives it to the first participant. The drinker claps once to receive the drink and downs the whole cup in one gulp. Everybody then claps three times, and the cup is passed back to the server. The same ritual takes place again until every participant has had his drink. When the bowl is empty, the mixer announces, "The bowl is empty, my chief," runs his hands around it again, and claps three times. This signifies the end of the ceremony. The whole ceremony unfolds in silence. A second bowl may be mixed and drunk, but with less solemnity. After the first bowl, conversation is allowed.

On another island, villagers catch a large type of mullet, a fish that is usually found in freshwater lakes. Once a year, clad in skirts made from leaves, the participants jump into the lake and stir up the water. This activity causes the fish to leap into the air, whereupon they are readily caught in the villagers' nets.

More commonly practiced throughout the islands is the fish drive. The whole village forms a large circle around the flat surface of a reef at rising tide. Holding a giant hoop made of vines and leaves, they slowly close the ring as the tide comes in, all the while singing, shouting, and beating the water with long poles. The fish are trapped in the circle and are easily driven toward a net near the shore.

One of the most solemn traditions is the presentation of the *tabua* (TAM-bwah). The tabua is a carefully shaped and polished whale tooth and is one of the most precious objects in Fiji. Once exchanged between chiefs as a sign of peace, today the tabua is presented as a sign of welcome or as a ceremonial prelude to doing business. In villages they are used in arranging marriages, expressing sympathy at funerals, asking for favors, or settling disputes. Fijians

Britain's Prince Harry (*right*) accepts a whale-tooth necklace at a farewell ceremony at Nadi Airport in October 2018. The prince and his wife, the Duchess of Sussex, stopped in Fiji as part of their official visit to Australia and the South Pacific.

believe that tabuas are the dwellings of ancestor spirits and, if buried with the dead, will protect them on their own journey to the afterworld.

EDUCATION

Fiji has a good educational system, with a high literacy rate of 93.7 percent. Education is free and compulsory from primary to secondary levels, with the Ministry of Education overseeing all schools, most of which are run by local committees or religious groups. In theory, public schools are culturally and racially diverse. However, the schools reflect the geographic distribution of ethnic groups and income levels, and therefore tend to be segregated in practice.

Almost all children attend primary and secondary schools. Primary school lasts six years. In the first three years, the medium of instruction is the child's mother tongue. Most iTaukei school kids are taught in the Bauan dialect, the dominant dialect in the country. Indian children are taught in either Hindi

The Dravuni Primary School on Dravuni Island.

(for Hindus) or Urdu (for Muslims). The Chinese community also runs its own schools, while European children are taught in English. English becomes the main medium of instruction for everyone in the fourth year of school and beyond.

Secondary school lasts another six years. At the end of the sixth year, students take the Fiji School Leaving Certificate exam, which will sort out whether they go on to a tertiary or a vocational institution. Students can stay on for a seventh year and take the Fiji Seventh Form Exam. This is the equivalent of the freshman year in university.

Higher education is available at the University of the South Pacific (USP) in Suva. USP is an center of higher education supported by twelve South Pacific countries. There is another campus in Western Samoa, where the School of Agriculture is located. The Suva campus offers courses in the humanities, sciences, and economics. The university has more than ten thousand students, who come from most South Pacific nations, except for Papua New Guinea and the French and American territories. Established in 2005, the University of Fiji at Lautoka, Viti Levu, is strongest in business studies, the humanities, science and technology, and law. The Fiji Institute of Technology offers courses in engineering, commerce, design, and hospitality and tourism.

In addition, a number of technical and vocational institutions recruit those wishing to learn a trade or skill. Many of these institutions are run by religious affiliates, but the government has increased its investment in technical education, realizing its growing importance.

SOCIAL PROBLEMS

The main problem engaging the Fijian people is that of change. With modern development, a breakdown of communal living overcomes many young Fijians who are looking for work in the large towns, in particular Suva. Without the traditional support of their village community, many young adults live confused lives and end up in the center of various social problems.

Migration from rural areas to urban centers has increased over the years, resulting in overcrowded conditions in towns. Unemployment, inadequate

The city center of Suva, the capital of Fiji, sits close to the water's edge.

housing and educational facilities, and a rise in crime, especially thefts, can be attributed mostly to urban migration.

Suva faces a serious housing problem, with a growing homeless population. Around 12.5 percent of the population of Fiji cannot afford adequate housing, living in substandard and unstable structures that are easily collapsed by hurricanes and earthquakes. In 2016, at least two hundred illegal squatter camps were said to exist around the country, with people having limited access to clean water and electricity.

Those living in housing projects provided by the Housing Authority of Fiji do not fare much better. Although they have a sound roof over their heads and proper sanitation, they face the usual problems associated with such projects: crime, alcoholism, vandalism, and antisocial behavior. Domestic abuse, called "wife-bashing" in Fiji, is on the rise.

Alcoholism and gambling are fast becoming leading problems. With kava drinking deeply entrenched in the lifestyle of most Fiji Islanders, alcoholism is one of the scourges that the churches are struggling to contain. Lotteries are very popular in Fiji, and it is even possible to place bets on Australian horse races at betting shops in cities. Extreme betting dips into household cash.

DENGUE FEVER

A recurring tropical disease that plagues Fijians is dengue fever. Since the illness is spread by mosquitoes, it tends to occur mostly in the rainy season, from November through April. Mosquitoes breed in pools of standing water, which easily accumulate during the wet season in discarded items such as used tires and empty containers.

The illness is caused by a virus, and symptoms typically begin five to seven days after being infected. A sudden high fever with severe headache and muscle pains—much like the flu—are the usual symptoms. Others include nausea, vomiting, and skin rash. Another name for the disease is 'break-bone fever' because that's what it feels like. Many people will get better within a week, but complications can take the disease to a more hazardous level. Danger signs that the illness may quickly turn fatal include severe stomach pain, continuous vomiting, blood in the vomit, fast breathing, bleeding gums, unexplained bruising, and a blotchy rash. At that point, hospitalization is critical.

In 2018, between January 1 and March 8, there were 1,854 recorded cases of dengue in Fiji, but that figure covers only a few months. In 2017, there were 2,699 known cases, and nine deaths.

There is no cure or preventive vaccine, though several vaccines are being studied in clinical trials. Although dengue fever is found in tropical regions around the world, it is particularly common to the Pacific Islands, where the incidence appears to be increasing, partly as a result of climate change.

HEALTH CARE

Fiji's population lives in generally good health, although the rise in alcoholism, sexually transmitted diseases, diabetes, and malnutrition is worrisome. In fact, in 2012, the top three causes of death as reported by the World Health Organization (WHO) were ischemic heart diseases, diabetes, and stroke. These diseases are all linked with growing economic affluence and a changing diet and lifestyle, and the health authorities are trying to educate the population about them. The government is also concentrating on improving environmental health, such as providing better sanitation and an improved water supply.

Although some of the worst tropical diseases, such as malaria, have been eliminated in Fiji, several communicable illnesses continue to be problematic.

A young man wears a traditional *sulu* for a dance performance on Robinson Crusoe Island.

Zika virus and dengue fever, both caused by mosquitoes, are dangerous illnesses for which there are, as yet, no cures or vaccines. Tuberculosis (TB) is a potentially fatal infection that most commonly affects poor people living in crowded, unclean conditions. The good news is that the incidence of TB in Fiji fell by three-quarters from 1990 to 2012, and the mortality rate of those who had the disease also dropped significantly. Nevertheless, it is still a problem; in 2011, there were 213 known TB cases in Fiji.

The public health-care infrastructure in Fiji is not on par with that of wealthier developed nations, but it compares favorably with most Pacific Island states. In general, it is much better in urban regions than in rural areas. There are three national hospitals, sixteen sub-divisional hospitals, and a number of health centers and nursing stations around the country. However, people in some rural areas still rely on traditional healers.

In addition, there are several private health-care groups with two private hospitals and a number of private day clinics and medical providers. Wealthier citizens and most expatriates living in the country use these private systems.

Public health care is not free but is generally inexpensive for those who can access it. However, Fiji suffers a serious lack of doctors and nurses. And mental health care is extremely limited.

FIJIAN DRESS

The traditional ethnic Fijian garment for both men and women is the *sulu* (SOO-loo), a wraparound skirt, or sarong. Traditionally made of *masi* (MAH-sih), or bark cloth, sulus are now made of industrial cotton. Men wear their sulus midcalf, while women wear them down to the ankles. Formal or ceremonial occasions call for more geometric patterns and muted colors. A short sulu is part of the Fijian military uniform. Grass skirts are worn during traditional observations, such as yaqona ceremonies and dance performances for tourists. The costumes are made of plain dyed grass and feature flowers as ornaments.

Most Indian women wear the sari, both in town and rural areas. The outfit consists of a short blouse called a *choli* (CHOH-lih) and a long length of cloth wrapped around as a skirt, with one end draped over the left shoulder or the head. Muslim women and those of north Indian origin opt for a long-sleeved tunic over a pair of straight pants. Indian men rarely wear the traditional dhoti, or loincloth, except during religious ceremonies.

Most men in Fiji wear the *bula* shirt. Resembling the Hawaiian aloha shirt, the bula is made of cotton and comes in a variety of colors. Floral patterns are most common, especially the hibiscus.

A Fijian man offers a hearty "Bula!" greeting on Nanuya Lailai Island, part of the Yasawa Group.

INTERNET LINKS

http://www.health.gov.fj/wp-content/uploads/2018/03/Protecting-Human-Health-from-Climate-Change.pdf
This report looks at the effects of climate change on health in Fiji, including the incidence of dengue fever and other climate-sensitive diseases.

https://www.nytimes.com/2017/04/11/world/asia/suva-fiji-tabua.html
This engaging article relates the role of the tabua in Fijian life.

https://www.telegraph.co.uk/news/worldnews/australiaandthepacific/fiji/1446723/Fijians-killed-and-ate-a-missionary-in-1867.-Yesterday-their-descendants-apologised.html
This is the story of the village that apologized for the cannibalism of Thomas Baker.

https://www.usp.ac.fj
This is the site of the University of the South Pacific.

RELIGION

A cross adorns a lush hillside on a Taveuni Island palm tree plantation.

8

I N INDIGENOUS FIJIAN RELIGION, WHEN a man died, his wife was strangled to accompany him to the afterlife. Happily for Fijian women, that tradition is no longer in practice. Though some traces of the indigenous ways remain, Christianity is now the religion of most iTaukei. The native Fijian population has been Christian ever since the early missionaries managed to convert King Cakobau in the mid-nineteenth century. Indian laborers brought Hinduism and Islam to the islands and their descendants have retained them to this day. Today, freedom of religion is guaranteed by the constitution.

Christians form 64.5 percent, Hindus make up 27.9 percent, and Muslims 6.3 percent. The rest of the population consists of Sikhs, 0.3 percent, and others, 0.3 percent. Only 0.8 percent of the whole population claims no religion at all.

The Fiji Islanders are very devout people, whatever their faith. Every village or settlement, however small, has at least one church or temple. Religious activities form an integral part of the national lifestyle, and religious ceremonies are performed with the utmost reverence.

Hindus worship with offerings of fruit, flowers, and camphor. Chanting and the beating of drums are used to acclaim the divine. Fasting and abstaining from meat are other means to attaining a holy state.

CHRISTIANITY

The largest religion by far in Fiji is Christianity. Almost all iTaukei and 2 percent of Fiji Indians belong to a Christian denomination. The major denominations are Methodist and Roman Catholic. The Methodists are the most powerful among the Christian groups in Fiji, with more than three-quarters of Fijian Christians belonging to this denomination. Among smaller churches are the Anglicans, Presbyterians, and Seventh-Day Adventists. The Mormons (Latter-Day Saints), along with several evangelical sects, are newer arrivals who call on foreigners to disseminate their messages. With the Pacific Theological College and the Pacific Regional Seminary located in Suva, Fiji is a sort of Pacific Islands Bible Belt. The South Pacific is one of the few areas in the world where there is a surplus of ministers of religion.

The first missionaries from the London Missionary Society arrived in Fiji in the 1830s to make converts to Christianity and to preach against cannibalism. They did not have much success until it dawned on them that they had to

A Catholic church in the town of Lautoka.

FIRE WALKING

Hindus perform a fire-walking ritual as part of the process of spiritual cleansing. Generally practiced by Indians from southern India, this annual ritual takes place on a Sunday between May and September, to coincide with a full moon. For ten days before the fire walking, participants remain isolated and eat only unspiced vegetarian meals. Rising early and going to sleep late, they spend their time praying and meditating. Spiritually readied at the end of the period, with their faces now smeared with yellow turmeric powder, they make their way to the sea or the nearest river for a bath. The priest chants selected prayers and pierces their cheeks, tongues, and bodies with metal skewers. Now in a trance, the fire walkers dance back to the temple grounds where the fire walking takes place.

Prior to the ceremony, a pit has been prepared with charred wood raked over glowing coals. Following the rhythm of chanting and frenetic drumming, each participant walks five times over the burning pit while being whipped by helpers. They feel no pain, and the soles of their feet do not get burned. Fire walking is the ultimate triumph of mind over body.

Native Fijians also have a fire-walking ceremony that is performed only by members of the Sawau tribe on Beqa Island, just off the south coast of Viti Levu. According to a tribal legend, a warrior was accorded the ability to walk on fire by a spirit-god that he had caught when fishing and then set free. The warrior's descendants act as high priests during the ceremony. Just as with the Hindus, Fijians taking part in fire walking have to purify themselves for two weeks prior to the ceremony. They walk on heated stones, however, instead of hot embers. Only men are allowed to perform this native Fijian ceremony, while the Hindu fire walking is also done by women.

The pit used is circular, with a diameter of 12 feet (3.7 m), and the stones are heated until they are white hot. The fire walkers prepare themselves in a nearby hut. Accompanied by much chanting, they come out and one by one briskly walk around the inside of the pit. After all of the men have had their solo turn, leaves and grass are thrown onto the stones, and all the walkers jump back inside the steaming pit while singing a farewell song.

Today, most fire walking in Fiji is performed mostly for tourists in resort hotels. For many native people, the Fijian fire-walking ritual has lost all its spiritual significance. As for the Hindu fire walking, many tour operators organize trips for tourists to watch it.

convert the chiefs first. The first such conversion occurred in 1839 when a high chief adopted Christianity, together with all his villagers and the other minor chiefs under his influence. The turning point came in 1854 when Chief Cakobau realized that he had to become a Christian in order to secure the cooperation of the Christian king of Tonga. Many chiefs converted because they were impressed by the guns and machines of the Christian Europeans. Besides, the Christian concept of a supreme God was similar to the Fijians' own traditional ideas of divinity. Many Fijians continued to worship their own gods and ancestor spirits even after converting to Christianity.

Christianity is all-pervasive in the Fijians' lifestyle. Christians attend church religiously. Most people who attend the city churches dress up to go to Sunday Mass—women in white dresses and hats, and men in plain, long-sleeved shirts and dark pants. Church attendance is high, as all Sunday activities revolve around the church community. At least one church or temple stands in each village or small town, and spiritual leaders are very influential and held in high esteem. Church choral singing is outstanding and fervent.

Fijians walk up stairs to the Methodist church in a village on Vanua Levu.

HINDUISM

The indentured Indian laborers brought Hinduism to Fiji. Hindus generally keep their worship to themselves and have not converted any native Fijians. As those who were shipped in to work in Fiji were all poor, lower-caste laborers, knowledge of Hindu historical philosophy is at best fragmentary among Fijian Hindus. In general, wealthier Indians tend to be less religious.

Hindus believe in one supreme power, who takes on different forms and names in order to be understood. He can be both life-giving and destructive. The aim of the Hindu devotee is to appease the destructive manifestations while imploring favors from the life-giving ones. Hindus believe in serial reincarnation and that everyone will have to face the consequences of their past deeds. In order to break out of the cycle of reincarnations and attain nirvana, where pain and care are banished, they must lead a moral life. Their main path to holiness is through religious asceticism—austere self-denial. Most Hindu homes have a small shrine for family worship. Each Indian village has at least one temple, but there is no fixed day for worship.

The richly decorated Hindu temple in Nadi is a colorful sight.

INDIGENOUS FAITHS

Prior to the arrival of the Christian missionaries, Fijians believed in a cadre of gods and spirits that had to be appeased and thanked. Most spirits tended to be malevolent, and they had to be kept happy so that they would not vent their wrath on the people. Fijians also performed ancestor worship, and the

souls of outstanding ancestors were morphed into local deities. Thus a war hero could become a god of war, while a successful farmer could become a god of plenty.

Chiefs and high priests were worshipped as representatives of the gods. Priests also served as the gods' mouthpieces. Idolatry took the form of worshipful attention to relics and carved whale teeth. The people offered food and kava roots for important rituals. They also practiced human sacrifice and mutilation.

Modern-day Fijians no longer practice their ancient faiths. But despite more than a century of Christianity, traces of ancestor and spirit worship can still be found in Fijians' attitudes. The hereditary chiefs are still regarded as some sort of supernatural beings, although the Fijians have been taught that all humans are the same. The singing and enacting of rituals in church are other examples of the fusion of indigenous faiths with Christian practices.

Chief Ratu Filimoni Nawawabalavu, dressed in a traditional *masi* made of *tapa* cloth, holds an offering of whale teeth at a ceremony in Nabutautau.

OTHER RELIGIONS

The descendants of Indian immigrants, particularly the Gujarati traders from western India, Fijian Muslims believe in one God and follow the religious teachings of the Prophet Muhammad as set down in the Quran, the Islamic holy book. They are a conservative community who lead a strict lifestyle, with many dietary restrictions. One of these is a ban on the consumption of alcohol. Young Muslims in Fiji are more liberal, however, and some even enjoy a drink of kava from time to time.

Sikhs came from northern India. Believing in a combination of Hinduism and Islam, Sikh men are highly noticeable with their unshaved facial hair and turbans wound around their heads.

Buddhists are mainly Chinese. Worshipping Buddha, Buddhists believe in attaining enlightenment, a condition of immortality that will put an end to all personal suffering. The Buddhists have a temple in Suva and run a few learning centers for Chinese children.

The Hindu deity Shiva adorns the Sri Siva Subramaniya Temple in Nadi.

INTERNET LINKS

https://blog.alienadv.com/fire-walking-fiji
The legend of the fire walkers and the contemporary ceremony is explained on this site.

http://fijisun.com.fj/2017/08/21/editorial-constitution-protects -religious-freedom
This editorial in the *Fiji Sun* touches on some of Fiji's current issues of religious freedom and tolerance.

https://www.state.gov/documents/organization/281066.pdf
This is the 2017 US State Department report on religious freedom in Fiji.

LANGUAGE

A man reads a newspaper outside Suva Cathedral.

9

BEFORE 1997, ENGLISH WAS THE only official language of Fiji. When Fiji was a British colony, the use of Fijian was discouraged by the authorities in favor of English, but the indigenous language reasserted itself after independence. With the adoption of the 1997 constitution, Fijian finally became a co-official language, along with English and Fijian Hindi. In 2005, a movement began that called for the elevation of the status of the indigenous language. Proponents want to see Fijian become the national language common to all, and required in schools. However, as of 2018, Fijian was still not a compulsory subject in schools, as English was, and many adults could not speak it. Some fear the Fijian language will be lost to future generations if it is not reinforced now.

Fijian is a VOS language, meaning verb-object-subject. Linguists use this term to describe the word order of a typical sentence in this type of language. This equates to sentences like "plays the flute Michael."

Although English is one of the official languages of Fiji, it is not the mother tongue of most Fiji Islanders. Many people in Fiji are bilingual, or even trilingual. At home, Fijians may speak a dialect of the Fijian language, and Indians speak Hindi or Urdu. Nevertheless, everybody learns English at school, and all Fiji Islanders have at least a working knowledge of English. All official matters are conducted in English.

FIJIAN

The Fijian language belongs to the enormous Austronesian language family that spans half the globe. Fijian accounts for more speakers than any other indigenous language in the Pacific. Many languages in Polynesia—Tongan, Samoan, Hawaiian, and Tahitian—are historically related to Fijian. Fijian spelling, however, differs from the languages of its neighbors.

Out of more than three hundred regional varieties spoken in Fiji, the Bauan dialect is regarded as the standard form of the language. In 1835 two Methodist missionaries, David Cargill and William Cross, devised a written form for the language, which until then had existed only in oral form. Cargill and Cross selected the Bauan dialect to represent the country because of the political and military supremacy of the island of Bau at that time. When they published a dictionary and a grammar, and translated the Bible into this dialect, the dominance of Bauan became entrenched. This is the dialect used in conversation by Fijians from different areas, in schools, and on the radio.

HINDI

Hindi, locally called Hindustani, is the language spoken by most Indians in Fiji. Although Muslim immigrants used Urdu and South Indian immigrants spoke Tamil or Telegu, their descendants today can also converse in Hindi. Some Muslims may have retained Urdu as their household or primary school language, but they have adopted Hindi for practical reasons.

The Hindi heard in Fiji actually is not the pure form spoken in India. Rather, it is a mixture of the various Indian dialects brought by the early immigrants. One of its main components is Bhojpuri, the dialect of Central India. Many

English words, such as "room," "towel," and "airport," have also made their way into Fijian Hindi. Some words have taken on slightly different meanings, however. The noun "book," for example, also includes magazines and other forms of print. Understandably, no Fijian word is found in Hindi vocabulary. Hindi script does not use the roman alphabet but employs a set of symbols representing forty-two different sounds. Indian children learn standard Hindi or Urdu in school, along with English.

FIJIAN PRONUNCIATION

Fijian spelling is based on the orthography created in 1835 by the missionaries David Cargill and William Cross. Some letters are pronounced differently from their English counterparts. Fijian has no pure *B*, *C*, or *D* sounds as in English. Vowels, however, are quite straightforward. Similar to other Pacific languages, the five vowels are pronounced in the same way as in Romance languages (such as Spanish or Italian). Each vowel is pronounced separately.

Vowels can be short or long. The longer form usually takes twice as long to say as the shorter vowel. The short forms are:

- A as in "f*a*ther"
- E as in "b*e*t"
- I as in "mach*i*ne"
- O as in "*o*ccur"
- U as in "z*oo*"

A long vowel can have a mark above it called a macron, as in *mamã*. To pronounce a word correctly, it is important to note the length of the vowel sound. For example, *mama* means "a ring," *mamã* means "chew it," and *mãmã* means "light." The word *mãmã* is pronounced twice as long as *mama*.

Consonants with unique pronunciations are:

- B —pronounced "mb" as in "me*mb*er"
- C —pronounced "th" as in "fa*th*er"
- D —pronounced "nd" as in "ha*nd*"
- G —pronounced "ng" in "si*ng*er"
- J —pronounced as a slurred "ch"
- Q —pronounced "ng" in "fi*ng*er"

The consonants *K*, *P*, and *T* are pronounced the same as in English, although they are much softer, and *R* is always rolled. The letter *V* is pronounced with the lower lip against the upper lip, somewhere between a *V* and a *B*.

Fijians always stress the next to last syllable. Some long words with four or five syllables also take a secondary stress. Not as apparent as the penultimate stress, the secondary stress usually falls on the first or second syllable.

ENGLISH

A major legacy of the British colonial rule is English, one of the official languages of Fiji. Although used mainly in written form rather than spoken, it is understood by almost everybody. All schools teach in English after the third grade. In a country with two main racial groups, English functions as a lingua franca—a third language that allows speakers of the two main languages to

A Peace Corps volunteer teaches English to Fijian children in a small village school.

understand one another. Fijians and Indians usually communicate with each other in English. Most forms of mass media use English, since they reach out to both communities.

Although Fiji Islanders learn British English at school, the way they speak English is influenced by the language they use at home. The Fijian accent is melodious and quite singsong. After more than a century, the English language in Fiji has evolved only slightly, with some words or phrases taking on different meanings. For example, the word "step" means to cut classes. When a Fijian says, "Good luck to you," it does not bear the good wishes usually associated with the phrase. Instead, it means, "Serves you right!"

MEDIA AND COMMUNICATIONS

Most Fijians, especially those on the outer islands, get their news from newspapers and radio. However, internet usage is growing, with an estimated 425,680 users, or about 46.5 percent of the population, in 2016. However, only one in one hundred inhabitants subscribed to broadband services in 2017.

NEWSPAPERS In the wake of the 2006 military coup, press freedom was severely curtailed, and journalists complained of human rights abuses committed against them by the authorities. The military government stationed censors in newsrooms to make sure that no story critical of the takeover was published.

Although freedom of expression is guaranteed in the Fijian constitution, press freedom has different meanings for the government and the media. The conservative faction of the population and the government itself fear that Western-style media opinions would unsettle the Fijian cultural heritage and harmony. At the same time, the government wants to use modern forms of communication to disseminate information and to promote development.

In 2010, the government issued a controversial media decree and established the Media Industry Development Authority of Fiji to oversee and regulate the media. The decree provides for tough penalties to be levied against media outlets that criticize the government. Although the Fijian government officially

SEDITION OR SIMPLY STRONG WORDS?

In 2018, the Fijian government charged the Fiji Times *with sedition, which means inciting rebellion against the government. As defined by the court in this particular case, sedition "is a crime against the State, or the authority of the government … Sedition covers everything, whether by words, deeds, or writing, which is calculated to disturb the tranquility of the State and leads ignorant persons to endeavour to subvert the government and the laws of the State."*

The government alleged that a letter to the editor published by the newspaper in its Nai Lalakai *vernacular version in 2016 promoted hostility between Muslims and non-Muslims in Fiji. The newspaper, its publisher, two editors, and the letter writer stood trial before the High Court in Suva.*

The prosecution charged that the letter said Muslims "are land-grabbing monsters who rape, murder, and abuse children," and that they would take over Fiji just as they had done in Bangladesh. The defense claimed the letter said no such thing, and that the inflammatory language was a mistranslation of the iTaukei language to English.

The verdict hinged on whether the letter writer's—and the newspaper's—intentions were to incite national instability. In the judgment, the court found the defendants not guilty, saying, "Deeply held political convictions frequently provoke strong emotions but there is authority to show that even strong or intemperate words or actions may not demonstrate a sedition intention if done with the purpose of expressing legitimate disagreement with the government of the day … The Courts should always be reluctant to extend any inroads on the protected constitutional freedoms."

Despite the vindication of the defendants, some observers claimed the trial was a government tactic to intimidate journalists. "It has become quite obvious that the government of Fiji has continued to charge people with sedition to suppress freedom of speech and also political dissent," said the letter writer's attorney, Aman Ravindra-Singh. "This particular case and outcome is a huge victory for the people of Fiji."

ended censorship of news content in 2012, the decree remains in place and continues to have a chilling effect on reporting. Fiji does not have a freedom of information law, and access to government information can be difficult for journalists to obtain.

Freedom House, a nonprofit organization that rates the status of press freedom in various nations, gave Fiji the status of "Partly Free" in 2017, with a score of 44/100, with 0 being the most free and 100 being the least free. That score was an uptick over recent previous years—in 2015, for example, Fiji's score was 52, so the trend at this writing is improving. However, in 2003—2004, the country's press was determined to be "Free," with a much better score of 29. (For comparison, in 2017, the press freedom score of the United States was 23, for a rating of "Free." However, at that point it was trending toward "less free.")

The main newspaper in Fiji is the English-language *Fiji Times*. Founded in 1869, it is Fiji's oldest newspaper. The *Times* also publishes the weekly *Nai Lalakai*, a Fijian-language paper. The only Hindi newspaper is a weekly, *Shanti Dut* ("Peaceful Messenger").

RADIO AND TELEVISION Fiji has two national radio networks. The government-sponsored Fiji Broadcasting Commission runs six radio stations—

two each in Fijian, Fijian Hindi, and English. Of the two English stations, one focuses on news and community issues while the other features music and chat. Bula FM specializes in Fijian music. Recordings of local singers are frequently aired by this station.

The independent provider Communications Fiji Limited broadcasts on five stations, one in Fijian, two in Fijian Hindi, and two in English. The latter are highly popular as they play English music interspersed with gossip. All five stations are mainly musical in content. In addition, Fijians can also tune in to several foreign stations, such as the BBC, Radio France, or Australia's ABC, as well as regional broadcasters playing Pacific Island music.

Fijian troops arrive at the offices of Fiji TV to monitor news reports during the period of military rule following the 2006 coup.

Television came to Fiji only in 1991, when Television New Zealand provided a live telecast of World Cup rugby matches. The main broadcaster is Fiji Television. Initially owned by the Fijian government and Television New Zealand, it is now a publicly listed company. Offering very little local content, the sole television station, Fiji One, airs mainly American sitcoms or other English-language shows sourced from the UK and New Zealand. Fiji One is on from midafternoon to early next morning. A clause in their license once forbade the station from broadcasting "anything offensive to the Great Council of Chiefs," but now that the council no longer exists, it's no longer relevant.

Digicel, an international telecommunications company headquartered in Jamaica, acquired the pay TV service Sky Pacific from Fiji Television in

2016. It offers twelve channels, two of which are Indian, showing Bollywood movies, and a single Chinese one. News channels such as CNN and BBC are also available. As with the print journalism, Fiji's radio and television are closely monitored by the authorities, and any reportage critical of the government is swiftly punished.

INTERNET LINKS

https://www.fijione.tv
This is the site of Fiji One television.

https://www.fijitimes.com/wp-content/uploads/2018/05/22.05.18 -HC-Crim-HAC-361.2016-State-v-Waqabaca-4-others-Judgment.pdf
The court judgment in the sedition trial of the *Fiji Times* is available as a PDF.

https://freedomhouse.org/report/freedom-press/2015/fiji
This organization provides a thorough look at government regulation of media freedom in Fiji.

http://www.mida.org.fj
This is the site of the Media Industry Development Authority, which includes the media decree of 2010 and a list of all media registered with MIDA.

https://www.omniglot.com/writing/fijian.htm
Omniglot provides a good introduction to the Fijian language.

https://www.tripsavvy.com/how-to-speak-the-fijian -language-1532878
This travel site offers pointers on pronunciation and some key words and phrases.

ARTS

A woman weaves a traditional palm mat on Kioa Island in Fiji.

10

I N KEEPING WITH A LONGSTANDING custom, Fiji's traditional arts and crafts are separated into women's work and men's work. Making pottery, weaving mats and baskets, and decorating bark cloth are the realms of female artisans. Woodcarving is strictly for men. Many villages have kept alive their traditional arts, although for some, the main purpose is to attract tourist money. While traditional arts are still very widely practiced in the country, Fijians have also adopted new and more modern forms of artistic expression.

Young artists are trying their hands at painting and experimenting with different styles. Fashion designers combine Fijian motifs and styles with modern technology. A popular motif used freely by contemporary fashion designers is the hibiscus, the national flower. Other artists have turned to photography, modern dance, and jazz.

Opened in 2009, the Fiji Center for the Arts in Suva provides a hub for collaboration with local and international artists. It is a focal point for dance, theater, music, fine art, crafts, and fashion, and the marketing of the arts, bringing together many diverse elements of Fiji's arts and crafts.

Fiji's premier music festival is the Uprising Festival of Music, Dance, and Lights held each November in Pacific Harbour. The beachside event presents twelve hours of nonstop music and dance, featuring more than one hundred artists. Musicians and dancers come from Fiji, Australia, and beyond for what is often called Fiji's "Party of the Year."

POTTERY

Fijian pottery is unique because most of the peoples in the South Pacific region had once forgotten how to make pots. Pottery making has been passed down by Fijian women for countless centuries, and different regions have different techniques and styles. Today's center of Fijian pottery is the Sigatoka Valley on Viti Levu, where the Lawai Pottery Village is a crafts center run by local women.

The pottery methods Fijians use are known as coiling and paddling. The potter cuts out a flat round piece of clay for the bottom of the pot. Using slabs of clay or coils and strips, she builds up the sides. Then she gently knocks the pot into shape with a wooden paddle. A smooth rounded stone inside the pot prevents the sides from caving in. The potter uses paddles of different sizes for different types of pots and for different areas of a single pot. When the potter is satisfied with the shape of the pot, she leaves it to dry indoors for a few days. When dry, the pot is taken outdoors and fired for an hour in an open pit. To seal the pots, a type of resin is applied on the outside surface when it is still hot. While enhancing its watertight capacity, the resin also gives a reddish sheen that brings out the color of the clay.

A woman and child make pottery in Nasilai Rewa village.

WOOD CARVING

Although most Fijians now use factory-made utensils and earthenware, the traditional *tanoa*, which is used for the daily drinking of kava in Fijian households, is still carved out of wood. Nowadays the tourist industry alone can keep Fijian woodcarving crafts alive. Many items are carved for sale as souvenirs, including those that are no longer used by the Fijian people, such as cannibal forks or war spears, and even artifacts that were never part of Fijian culture, such as Polynesian tikis (images) and masks.

LAPITA POTTERY

The ancient Lapita peoples were the common ancestors of today's inhabitants of Polynesia, Micronesia, and some areas of Melanesia. These seafaring peoples came originally from Southeast Asia around 1500 BCE and slowly spread eastward through the islands of Melanesia and out to the remote archipelagos of the central and eastern Pacific. By about 1000 BCE, they had reached Fiji.

Lapita pottery is named after an archaeological site in New Caledonia which was first discovered in the 1960s. Recovered from archaeological digs throughout the Pacific Ocean, Lapita pottery provides a way of dating the human settlement of the Pacific Islands, as well as how the populations of the region are related to one another.

Lapita is an ornately decorated style of pottery, usually covered in geometric patterns that were impressed into the clay prior to firing. Some artifacts display patterns made of dot-like incisions, much like those used in tattooing. The finest example is a clay head recovered in New Ireland, an island in Papua New Guinea. The pattern was made by a needle-fine, comb-like tool similar to those used by Polynesians in traditional tattooing. Lapita pottery has affinities with Asian pottery, evident in the shape of the jars, but the ornamental design is a local development.

One of the best known Lapita sites in Fiji is in the Sigatoka area, where sand dunes continue to unveil not only artifacts but also human bones. Other impressive pots have been found on Yanuca Island, at Natunuku, Naigani, and Lakeba.

Lapita pottery suggests a sophisticated society. By about 500 BCE, Fijian pottery characteristics changed to a simpler form. Patterns were no longer elaborate, as functionality and simplicity came to be valued more than mere aestheticism. This switch coincided with a shift in population and occupations. Agriculture had increased significantly, as the population continued to grow and expand into interior areas of the islands. Around the same time, intergroup warfare and cannibalism appears to have increased, and fortified villages became common. Potters turned to a straightforward variety of decorations that lasted from 100 BCE to 1000 CE. Pottery making continued throughout Fiji until the period of European contact.

Today, traditional pottery is made in only a few villages, and mainly for tourists.

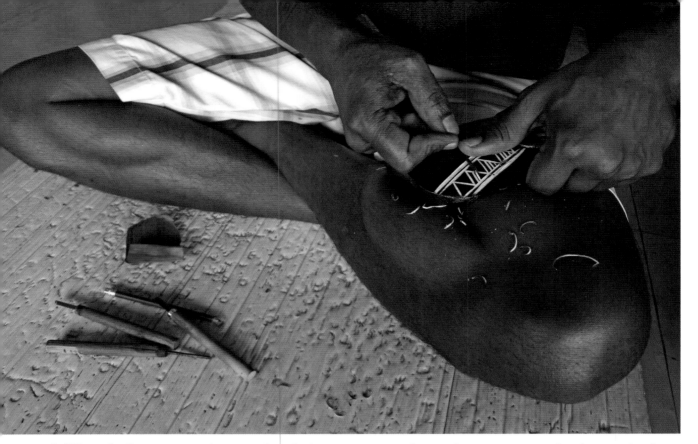

In Fiji, sea turtles symbolize good luck. Here, an indigenous man carves a sea turtle out of wood in 2016.

The people of the Lau Group have the reputation for being the best woodcarvers in Fiji. There are many different types of woodcarving. For example, human and animal forms are generally used for such religious objects as yaqona vessels. Items for religious uses are carved out of ironwood, which is considered sacred. Hibiscus wood is much lighter and more easily broken. In the old days, it took years to carve a war club, as the carving was done in the living tree and left to grow into a desired shape.

Today, woodcarvers use steel tools. Sometimes, they may rub shells over the carvings to give a fine polish to the most exquisite pieces. In areas where the Polynesian influence is strong, carved objects are inlaid with shell, ivory, or bone.

OTHER ARTS AND CRAFTS

Weaving is a craft that most village girls learn when young. In some tribes, only women can weave. The most common objects are mats, but baskets and hats are also made. Woven items make popular wedding or baptismal presents and are also given to chiefs as a form of tribute. The usual weaving material is pandanus leaf, but coconut husks, banana stems, vine tendrils, and waterweeds are also used. The traditional method for blackening the leaves for contrasting color patterns was to bury them in mud for several days and then boil them with certain other leaves. Today, most weavers use chemical dyes.

Another traditional craft that is almost exclusively the domain of women is making *masi* (MAH-sih). Masi, also called *tapa* in Polynesia, is the traditional pounded bark cloth used in Fijian rituals. Masi feels like felt. When the cloth is ready, geometric patterns are applied with stencils made from green pandanus and banana leaves. Traditional dyes are rust, obtained from red clay, and black, made from an infusion of candlenut and mangrove bark. Plain masi is beige.

LITERATURE

Fijians have a very long tradition of storytelling. Myths and legends are passed down from one generation to another in informal storytelling gatherings or around a shared bowl of kava. These stories recount the origins of the Fijian people or explain the nature of plants and animals. One legend is that the coconut has three "eyes" or indentations at the bottom in order to watch out for people below the tree so that it does not drop on them. Traditional stories live in an oral tradition. Apart from some English translations, they have not been written down into books for Fijian children to read or learn. Fortunately, many Fijians still live in traditional villages, so this folklore is not yet in danger of being lost.

Fijian literature is mostly written in English. Although the local literary community is rather small, it is made up of many talented and committed

A library in Suva

Meke *(MAY-keh)* is a traditional performance combining song, dance, and theater. Reenacting legends and stories from Fijian history, mekes were arranged for entertainment and also to welcome visitors or to mark important occasions. Traditional mekes were handed down from one generation to the next, and new ones were composed for specific occasions. Before the missionaries arrived, mekes involved some manner of spiritual domination, with the possessed participants dancing and chanting in a trance.

Men, women, and children take part in a meke, although the sexes perform different dances. When they dance together as in the tralala *(trah-LAH-lah)*, which is a two-step shuffle, men and women dance side by side. Another dance with both sexes participating is the vakamalolo *(vah-KUH-mah-LOH-loh)*, which is performed seated on the floor. Men usually perform war dances. Dressed in grass skirts and with their faces painted black by charcoal, the warriors form a line while brandishing clubs and spears. In the areas where Tongan influence is strong, paddles are also used as accessories. The women's dance is called seasea *(SEE-see)*. Dressed in conservative sulus *and blouses, or mission dresses, they sing and dance gracefully with fans. All dancers wear flower necklaces, or leis, and women also adorn themselves with flowers in their hair.

In a Fijian meke, the seating arrangement is very important, just as every movement and gesture during the performance has a special significance. Even the spectators are expected to follow certain rules. Important guests are given special seating positions in order to avoid offense.

poets, playwrights, and writers. One of the foremost contemporary writers is Joseph Veramu, whose short story collection *Black Messiah* (1989) was well received in literary circles. His novel *Moving Through the Streets* (1994) offers a keen insight into the life of teenagers in Suva. Rotuma-born Vilsoni Hereniko, a leading playwright, wrote and directed Fiji's first, and so far only, feature film, *The Land Has Eyes* (2004).

Indian writers express themselves in both Hindi and English. A central thread lacing through all their works is the theme of injustice and the plight of indentured laborers. Prominent Indian writers are Subramani, Satendra Nandan, Raymond Pillai, and Prem Banfal.

SINGING

Fijians love to sing! Songs express a large part of the people's oral tradition. In the villages, local legends are retold through songs. When the missionaries came to Fiji, they introduced hymns and choral singing, which the natives readily embraced. Singing is a traditional island activity, and the villagers felt a close affinity for Christian lyrics and music. Even the smallest village church

Chorus members wear traditional dress as they sing at an event on Malolo Island.

boasts a choir, and Sunday service singing is fervent and of exceptional quality. Church music includes choices from both Western and traditional repertories, and hymns are sung in English and Fijian. In fact, many new lyrics have been written to traditional music. Although the title of Fiji's national anthem, "God Bless Fiji," resembles the British "God Save the Queen," the song took its music from an old Fijian melody. Nearly all traditional instruments have disappeared, and the most popular musical instrument today is the guitar.

Contemporary singers have also been influenced by modern trends, such as reggae and jazz. Popular performers appear in the major hotels and in nightclubs in Suva. Many of them have also recorded their music on CDs, which are sold in music stores.

As for the Indian community, they are more attracted to songs in Hindi from "Bollywood," the Indian movie industry based in the Indian megalopolis of Mumbai (Bombay). They like to listen to original recordings of movie music, usually a mixture of Western pop and Indian styles played with traditional and modern instruments. Local Indian singers have also started doing cover versions of popular songs. Indian bands perform Hindi songs at weddings and parties. Classical Indian music is less popular, although the cultural centers offer courses for the tabla, an Indian drum played in pairs, and sitar, a long-necked stringed instrument with a plaintive echoing sound, recognized the world around as "Indian."

ARCHITECTURE

The traditional Fijian house is the *bure*. Usually rectangular in shape, it is made of tightly woven bamboo walls with a thatched roof. In the past, tree fern trunks were used. In eastern Fiji, where Tongan and Samoan influence is strong, circular bures can also be found.

Bures are one-room dwellings with few windows and a low door. It is quite dark inside. The packed-earth floor is covered with pandanus mats, and a curtain at one end separates the sleeping area from the living room. Cooking is done in a separate, smaller bure. Except for numerous floor mats and some storage containers, the bure is bare of furniture, because its occupants sit and sleep on the floor.

Bure building is a traditional skill passed down from father to son. The dwelling is cheap and relatively fast and easy to build. When a family needs a new bure, the whole village takes a hand in its construction. Since the house is made of plant materials, the walls and roofs require regular maintenance. This does not mean, though, that the bure is a house that can be destroyed easily. It is usually sturdy enough to withstand hurricanes, common occurrences in the islands of Fiji.

A house in Navala village is an example of traditional bure architecture.

INTERNET LINKS

https://fijihighcom.com/education-and-culture
This site offers a quick overview of Fijian culture.

https://www.lonelyplanet.com/fiji/travel-tips-and-articles/from -ukuleles-to-reggae-fijis-music-scene
This travel site provides information about today's music scene in Fiji.

https://www.lostateminor.com/2014/07/03/fijians-create-amazing -traditional-masi-art
With many bright images, this article discusses the creation of a piece of masi artwork.

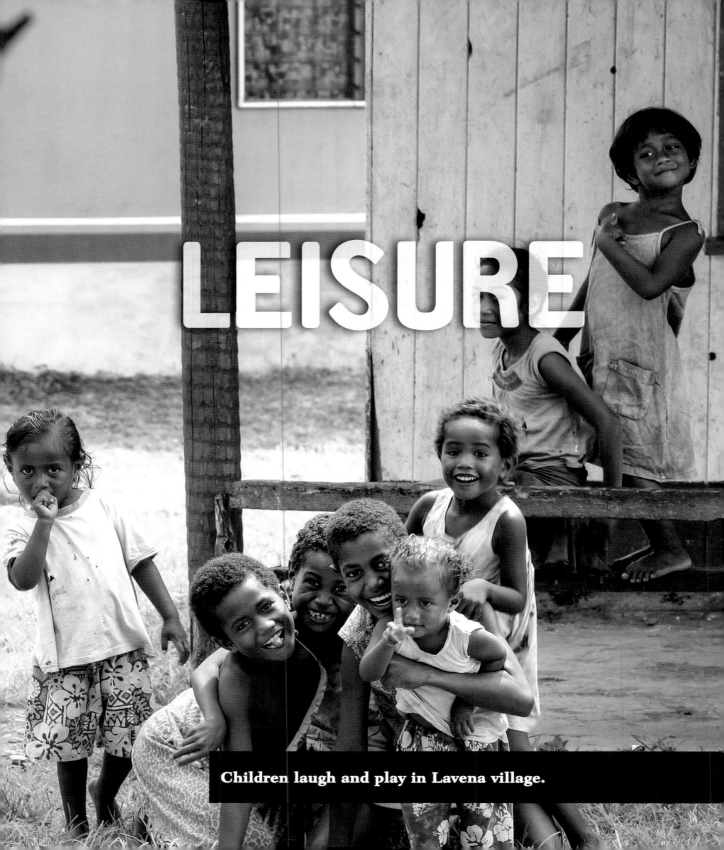

LEISURE

Children laugh and play in Lavena village.

I N FIJI, WESTERN FORMS OF LEISURE blend with traditional, communal activities. Most men spend their free time practicing or watching a Western sport, but their most popular pastime is drinking kava with a circle of friends. As for the women, spare time revolves around church and other communal activities. Chatting while working on a group project is probably the most engaging pastime.

Most people prefer to enjoy their time in a casual manner, so long as they have the ability to feed, clothe, and shelter their families. Because most leisure activities are simple and inexpensive, or even free, the Fijians do not have to work very hard to be able to afford the little cash needed for a good time.

For tourists, of course, there is another whole world of activities, and these may be quite pricey indeed. From action and adventure to history and culture to the ultimate in relaxation, there are plenty of offerings. Markets, spas, and restaurants cater to visitors with money. Cruises by ship, sailboat, canoe, or rafts are popular, along with nature hikes, water sports, and nightlife.

11

In Fiji, there is a rugby field in every village, and a game is played almost every week. There are about eighty thousand registered rugby players in the country—10 percent of the total population! The season lasts from April to September.

SPORTS

Fijians are very enthusiastic about sports, and they play all kinds. Sports are banned on Sundays, which are reserved for going to church. Golf is a diversion that has received a lot of international investment, with world-class facilities in some resorts. These posh operations attract mainly wealthy tourists to the islands. Not many Fijians are inclined to take up the game. Former Prime Minister Sitiveni Rabuka is an avid golfer, though, and it has been rumored that many political moves, including the 1987 coups, were plotted on the golf links.

Boys play rugby, a favorite sport.

Another sport that both locals and tourists love is scuba diving. With its astonishing wealth of coral reefs, Fiji is an important center for diving in the Pacific. Surfing has existed in Fiji for hundreds of years and is another popular activity with both locals and visitors. Windsurfing is also catching on and can be practiced now at more locations than surfing.

Rugby is the prime national pastime, and Fijians take great pride in the national team's achievements. A game similar to American football, it is played by teams of seven, ten, or fifteen players. The aim is to score points by touching the ball down between the opponent's goalposts. Rugby players need to be strong and hardy since it is a sport with lots of physical contact.

DRINKING

Drinking kava is hands down Fiji's most popular leisure pursuit. Both iTaukei and Indian Fijians are devoted to this pastime. Kava is not sold in bottles, as the drink has to be consumed as soon as it is prepared. Its elaborate preparation and the ritual surrounding drinking it is a way of buoying community spirit. Sharing a bowl of kava, with the soft strumming of guitars in the background,

THE BIG FIJIAN

Vijay Singh (b. 1963) is one of the world's top pro golfers. The Indo-Fijian athlete was born and grew up on the western coast of Viti Levu, back when Fiji was still a colony of the United Kingdom. He has said he played golf with little coconuts when he couldn't find golf balls. Singh's father was an avid golfer, and Vijay followed in his footsteps, going even further. He became a professional golfer in 1982 and won the Malaysian Open in 1984.

By 2004, he was the number-one golfer in the world. In 2006, he was inducted into the World Golf Hall of Fame. The 6-foot, 2-inch-tall (188 cm) Singh is sometimes called the Big Fijian, not only for his height but for his great achievement. He played well into his forties and holds the record for most PGA Tour wins after age forty. As he got older, however, injuries and age began to affect his game. In his fifties, he began playing in senior tournaments. In July 2018, he won the PGA Tour Champions Constellation Senior Players Championship at Exmoor Country Club in Illinois.

participants immediately feel relaxed and close, and a bond naturally forms among them. Drinking kava is the Fijian's link with his ancestral past, the ceremony and devotional ritual having originated in ancient Fijian society. Today, Fijians regard it more as a social activity than a religious rite, though its cultural value is very great.

In the villages, men and women do not drink kava together. The custom is for men to gather around a large bowl of the mix in a bure and talk while drinking. The women do the same, but they confine themselves to the kitchen. Some old women are allowed to join the men in their drinking sessions.

Kava is not an intoxicating liquor, so it does not make the drinkers drunk, and drinking sessions do not degenerate into drunken brawls. The brew is mildly narcotic, however, and the drinker usually feels reluctant to do any kind of work afterward. Its effects range from light-headedness to a mild rush of euphoria.

Although kava is consumed primarily as a social drink, local healers have used it to treat various ailments, such as tooth decay and respiratory diseases. Kava is also a diuretic, and pharmaceutical manufacturers use it in their formulas. Excessive drinking of kava causes numerous disorders, including

Rugby is Fiji's national sport and the Fiji Sevens team has won the Rugby World Cup Sevens twice, in 1997 and 2005. When Fiji won the World Cup for the first time, the whole country rejoiced with a public holiday, and the government generously financed national celebrations. The Fiji Sevens team has also been the victor of the Hong Kong Sevens Tournament—considered to be the world's premier sevens tournament—ten times since the competition started in 1976. With its win over South Africa in June 2009, Fiji established itself as the most successful team ever in the annual Hong Kong tournament.

But Olympic gold eluded Fiji until 2016. That was the first year the Olympics included rugby in its Summer Games. Fiji's teams in other sports, such as soccer, had never medaled, but rugby was, after all, Fiji's national game. Sure enough, the Fiji men's sevens team won the gold medal. The win was particularly satisfying for Fiji when it beat its former colonial ruler, Great Britain, by 43–7.

Back home, the country erupted in joy. Flag-waving fans danced in the streets and on rooftops from tiny villages to crowded Suva, and the government proclaimed a public holiday. The victory was a tremendous boost to the nation that was still recovering from the devastation of Cyclone Winston earlier that year.

loss of appetite, bloodshot eyes, lethargy, restlessness, stomach pains, and scaling of the skin. The latter condition is fairly common among heavy kava drinkers, who may consume up to 10 quarts (9.5 liters) or more daily!

Because of the congenial nature of the drinking, many business deals or contacts are made while sharing kava. There is always a bowl of kava in government offices for the staff to dip into during their breaks. Visitors are also offered a *bilo*, or cup. Most employees have their own bilo, which they keep at the office. In the old days, there used to be a bowl of kava in the back balcony of the parliament building for the legislators to share. Many police stations hold nightly kava drinking sessions when things are quiet. There are also stories of magistrates imbibing their favorite drink while hearing court cases.

Although beer and other types of liquor are available in Fiji, kava is the popular choice at social gatherings, parties, and religious ceremonies. Cultivation of the kava plant is a prosperous enterprise for farmers all over the archipelago.

Drinking alcohol is also done at private clubs, a relic behavior from colonial days. Although prominent signs proclaim, "Members Only," they are actually open to any well-dressed visitor. The drinks of choice in the clubs are beer and other liquor, not kava.

INTERNET LINKS

https://www.nytimes.com/2017/02/23/business/fiji-kava-prices -drink.html
This in-depth article about growing kava in Fiji features many large photos.

https://www.theguardian.com/sport/2016/aug/11/fiji-great -britain-rio-2016-rugby-sevens-final
The story of Fiji's Olympic gold in rugby is related in this article.

FESTIVALS

A man holds a torch as he performs a fire dance at night.

FIJI ISLANDERS CELEBRATE A NUMBER of sacred and secular occasions throughout the year. Important Christian, Hindu, and Muslim holy days—some somber and some joyful—are observed as public holidays. Regional festivals, such as the Hibiscus Festival in Suva and the Sugar Festival in Lautoka, attract tourists and provide colorful opportunities for music, dancing, and feasting. In addition, there are two government holidays.

CHRISTMAS AND EASTER

For Christians in Fiji—who make up the majority of the country's people—Christmas and Easter are the most important festivals in the year. Christmas celebrates the birth of Jesus Christ and Easter celebrates his resurrection, when, according to Christian belief, he returned to life after having died on the cross. On these holy days, many Christians will attend church.

CHRISTMAS On Christmas Eve, well-practiced church choirs sing beautiful carols, and the whole congregation joins in. Children, turned

12

Fiji's fire-walking ceremony—a popular tourist attraction—grew out of a five-hundred-year-old legend among the Sawau people of Beqa. Accordingly, only certain Sawau men are able to walk barefoot across red hot stones without suffering pain or visible injuries. Prior to the ceremony, the walkers must abstain from certain pleasures for about two weeks; failure to do so will result in burns to their feet.

out in their best clothes, happily look forward to this day, when they receive presents of toys and books from Santa Claus. Naturally, in Fiji's warm climate, the only "white Christmas" is found on the white sand beaches, where festive holiday parties often take place.

The Fijians' love of food is reflected in all their festive celebrations, so much feasting takes place during the holiday season. Kava and traditional Fijian dishes are the highlights at every table. Villages throw huge communal parties, while people in towns attend smaller gatherings at friends' homes or in hotels. Many parties feature *lovo* (LOH-voh), which is food cooked in a traditional underground pit.

In the British tradition, Fijians also observe Boxing Day on December 26. For the most part, it's a day to continue the merriment, with the religious obligations now over. Many Fijians go to the beach for picnics and parties. Besides an opportunity to unwind, this is also a time to think about the things they have done in the past year and prepare for the challenges ahead. It is also

Meat wrapped in palm leaves is ready to be cooked in the *lovo* pit.

As of 2019, Fiji celebrates ten official holidays a year. These are mainly historical and religious in context. Apart from fixed dates such as New Year's Day or Christmas, the other holidays are observed on a Monday or Friday so that everyone can benefit from a long weekend. In addition to national holidays, Fijians also take a day off from school or work to celebrate cultural festivals.

Each year, the government approves a calendar of official holidays for the upcoming year, and occasionally certain observances are added or deleted. One recent holiday that was removed from the 2019 calendar is National Sports and Wellness Day, which had been an official day off on June 29 from 2014 through 2018.

New Year's Day—January 1
Prophet Muhammad's Birthday—variable according to Islamic calendar
Good Friday—March/April
Easter Saturday—March/April
Easter Monday—March/April
Constitution Day—September 7
Fiji Day—2nd week of October
Diwali—October/November
Christmas Day—December 25
Boxing Day—December 26

a good time for family and friends to get together. The festive mood continues until New Year's Day, which is celebrated by everyone in Fiji. In some villages, the partying lasts for a week or even the whole month of January!

On Rotuma the local version of caroling is the Fara, a festival of dancing and revelry that begins on December 1 and continues through the month. Bands of young people wander from house to house in the evening, singing fara (traditional) songs, dancing, and clapping their hands. They are met with a sprinkle of talcum powder and perfume to ward off evil spirits, and may also be rewarded with little gifts of fruit. But if their singing is poor, the householders throw water on them to chase them away!

Candles are lit in celebration of Diwali, the Hindu festival of lights.

EASTER During Holy Week, which leads to Easter Sunday, pious Christians may take part in the Fijian Crosswalk. For this week-long spiritual processional, participants carry heavy wooden crosses on a 125-mile (200 km) pilgrimage across the island of Viti Levu, beginning in Suva, the capital, and ending in the town of Nadi. The walk symbolizes the suffering of Jesus Christ in the days leading to his crucifixion in Jerusalem. Good Friday through Easter Monday form a long weekend of Easter observances. The holy weekend is observed with feasting and, of course, the sharing of kava.

DIWALI

Diwali, the Hindu festival of lights, came to Fiji with the large influx of Indians in the nineteenth and twentieth centuries. It is a day to celebrate the triumph of light over darkness, and by extension, good over evil and knowledge over ignorance. The date of Diwali changes from year to year, but is usually observed on a moonless night in October or November, one of the darkest nights in the year.

Weeks before the festival, Hindu families start to clean their homes and prepare little oil lamps, candles, or special electric lights to decorate their homes. On the morning of Diwali, everyone puts on new clothes and distributes cakes and candies to neighbors and friends. Fruit and candies are also offered to Lakshmi, the goddess of wealth and beauty. Hindus believe that the goddess comes to visit earth on Diwali night following the lighting of the oil lamps and that she will enter only the homes that have been properly cleaned. In the evening, everyone gathers at the family shrine to recite prayers and make offerings to Lakshmi. The children's foreheads are daubed with red powder, and the women draw good-luck patterns with colored powders outside the front door. As night falls, the lamps are lit, and every Hindu home glitters with light.

THE HIBISCUS FESTIVAL

Started in 1956, the Suva Hibiscus Festival was originally based loosely on Hawaii's Aloha Week. The festival lasts more than a week in August and brings together cultural performances by local and foreign groups, a glamorous beauty pageant, and a charity fund-raising drive. Every year, the lord mayor of Suva declares the festival open, and a parade kicks off the celebrating, followed at night by a display of fireworks.

Fashion shows, food tasting, music, dancing, and games dominate this festival. One of the highlights is the Miss Hibiscus Pageant. The winner goes on to represent Fiji in the Miss South Pacific Pageant.

A daylong children's carnival caters to the youngsters. Babies are entered in a baby show, and prizes are awarded to the most adorable tots and their parents. Older children take part in an aerobics championship contest, and some of them participate in musical and dance performances and fashion shows. It is a fun-filled and lively carnival that many children happily await.

Since Fiji is largely a Christian country, no event is complete without a religious component. The Hibiscus Festival features singing competitions between very accomplished church choirs, and religious worship led by youth organizations and church groups. These exciting presentations usually draw many entrants.

OTHER ETHNIC FESTIVALS

Hindus also celebrate Holi, the Festival of Colors, in a big way. This festival marks the arrival of spring in India and is celebrated in February or March in Fiji, at the same time as spring in India. Indian villages are awash with color as everyone has a good time throwing colored water or powders on friends and neighbors. Whole neighborhoods dance in the streets, embrace each other, and exchange playful greetings.

In the Chinese community, Chinese New Year is celebrated with lion dances and much merrymaking. There is plenty of good food, and friends and relatives visit one another, wearing new clothes. Children receive red envelopes containing small amounts of money as a symbol of good luck.

Although it's not exactly a festival, Vula i Balolo, or the Rising of the Balolo, is a yearly event that villagers in the outer islands and coastal areas eagerly look forward to. Balolo is the Fijian name given to Eunice viridis, *also known as the edible palolo worm, which lives deep in the coral reef. Measuring about 12 inches (30 cm) in length, this sea worm looks like spaghetti underwater.*

Two nights a year, once in October and again in November, millions of balolo release their tails, which rise to the surface of the ocean to mate, turning the sea into a writhing mass of red, green, and brown. The villagers, who had been lying in wait in their boats, immediately pounce on the tails, scooping them up into buckets, wicker baskets, or plastic containers. To the Fijians, the balolo tails, full of either sperm or eggs, are rare delicacies, the taste of which recalls that of caviar. They can be eaten raw or fried. The villagers need to work fast, for the worm tails melt into a gooey mass with the first rays of the sun and sink back down to the bottom.

The traditional Fijian calendar can pinpoint the rising dates of the balolo with unerring accuracy. The first rising occurs in early October when only a few of these creatures appear, and the Fijians refer to it as Little Balolo. The next showtime, Big Balolo, happens at the high tide on the eighth day after the full moon in November, and whole villages pour out to feast.

When the balolo come up, shoals of fish converge onto the reefs, vying with the local villagers for their share of the delicacy. On Vanua Levu, Vula i Balolo coincides with the arrival of a small deep-sea fish called deu, *which swims up the mangrove estuaries to lay eggs. Women in the villages along the southeast coast gather in the rivers to catch the tasty fish.*

Muslim festivals are much less jubilant, being times to pray and strengthen relationships. Although the only official Muslim holiday in Fiji is the birth of the Prophet Muhammad, Muslims also celebrate Eid al-Fitr and Eid al-Adha. The former marks the end of Ramadan, the fasting month, and the latter commemorates the willingness of Abraham to sacrifice his son to God. All of these special occasions are dated according to the Muslim lunar calendar, and therefore the corresponding dates on the Western calendar change each year.

INTERNET LINKS

https://blog.alienadv.com/fire-walking-fiji/
The legend of the fire walkers and the contemporary ceremony is explained on this site.

https://www.fijimarinas.com/balolo-rising-in-fiji
This article takes an in-depth look at the rising of the balolo.

http://press-files.anu.edu.au/downloads/press/p301541/pdf/interlude-delicacy.pdf
This charming story is a first-person narrative about the rising of the balolo.

https://theculturetrip.com/pacific/fiji/articles/fiji-s-top-10-festivals-you-don-t-want-to-miss
This site provides short takes and photos about Fijian festivals.

https://www.timeanddate.com/holidays/fiji
This calendar site has up-to-date information about public holidays and observances in Fiji.

FOOD

A man sells eggplant at the Lautoka market.

13

A COUNTRY'S CUISINE IS OFTEN A clue to its history. This is true in Fiji, where the food brings together all the various influences from the country's diversified population. Fijian, Indian, Polynesian, Chinese, and Western cuisines can all be found in the country.

In the villages, the predominant ethnic groups usually keep to their traditional diets, but urban Fijians get to sample different types of foods. Suva and Nadi have all kinds of restaurants, catering to every taste and budget. Even American-style fast food has found its way to Fiji. No truly Fijian dish has evolved from the fraternity of so many culinary traditions. Only Chinese curries combine two separate cuisines—Chinese and Indian.

In general, only native Fijians and Indians eat with their hands. The other communities use spoons and forks. Very few people eat British style, with both a knife and fork used simultaneously. In the villages, meals are eaten on the floor, with the family sitting on mats. When entertaining, Fiji Islanders believe that they should provide enough for their guests to eat their fill—the result is usually too much food. Some hosts even wait for their guests to finish eating before starting on their own meals.

Fijians, Chinese, and Europeans do not have any dietary restrictions, eating the meats and vegetables available in the markets. The Indian community, however, deals with restrictions on what they are free to eat. Muslims do not eat pork and are not supposed to drink alcoholic beverages. Some young Muslim men, however, partake of kava and beer. As for Hindus, tradition encourages them to avoid eating beef, but this restriction is observed only in the most conservative families. Some Hindus are vegetarians.

Fijians enjoy eating foods made with taro leaves. The vegetable is nutritious and tastes something like spinach. However, unlike spinach, taro leaves can be poisonous in the raw and must be properly cooked before being consumed. Both the tuber itself and its leaves contain calcium oxalate, which can irritate the skin. Ingested, it causes severe irritation and can cause the throat to swell up, cutting off the air supply.

THE FIJIAN OVEN

A festive lovo *pit is prepared and decorated with flowers.*

The Fijian equivalent of the Hawaiian luau is called *lovo*. The whole village works together to prepare this feast. First, a large pit is dug and lined with a deep layer of dry coconut husks. The husks are set on fire, and once the fire is going well, stones are heaped on top. When most of the husks have burned away and the stones are very hot, the food, wrapped in banana leaves, is lowered into the pit. Fish and meat are the first to go in, then the vegetables are placed on top. Everything is covered with banana leaves and more hot stones, and the food is left to cook. After about two and a half hours, when everything is cooked, the top leaves and stones are removed.

A popular dish cooked in the lovo is *palusami* (pah-loo-SAH-mih). A mixture of canned corned beef with onions, tomatoes, and coconut cream, the palusami is wrapped in taro leaves before cooking. At times, a whole pig is cooked in the pit. The animal is cleaned and stuffed with banana leaves and hot stones. This method cooks the meat inside and out.

Lovos are still prepared in the villages for special occasions, such as the inauguration of a new chief or a wedding or for such grand festivals as Christmas Day. They are now more often organized in resort hotels, however, accompanied by a *meke* or a fire-walking ceremony.

STAPLES

The universal staple food in Fiji is rice, which is eaten by all the different ethnic groups. The country aims to be self-sufficient in rice by turning over large areas of sugarcane fields to rice cultivation, but more than a third of the total demand is still imported.

Indians also eat roti, a flat tortilla-like unleavened bread made of wheat flour and cooked on a griddle. As for the Fijians, a number of starchy roots and tubers go into their diet. Taro is usually boiled, but breadfruit, which is an important food that's found everywhere in the South Pacific, can also be baked or roasted. When cooked, breadfruit tastes like bread. Fijians also like to eat boiled yam, sweet potatoes, and cassava. *Vakalolo* (vah-kah-LOH-loh) is a sweet pudding made with all the starchy roots that Fijians eat. Mashed taro, cassava, and breadfruit are combined with coconut milk and caramelized sugarcane juice to make this special delicacy, which is usually served only at traditional feasts.

For protein, Fijians consume large amounts of lagoon fish that the families catch themselves. Fish is eaten raw, but marinated in lime juice which "cooks" the flesh, in a salad called *kokoda* (ko-KON-da); or baked in coconut cream with taro and cassava. Beef and pork are occasionally fried and eaten with these roots. Chicken, called "bird meat," is not very popular among Fijians. Exotic meats that are still consumed in Fiji include turtle and bat. Although turtles are an endangered species and are protected by law, turtle meat can still be found in the markets. Boiled bat, which most people today consider a foul-smelling and vile-tasting dish, used to be very popular in Fiji. Today, however, only the older generation tolerates it.

Hindus do not eat beef, and use lamb or goat meat cooked in spicy curries. Muslims, on the other hand, don't eat pork, and cook their curries with beef. Indians also consume large amounts of yellow or red lentils. Cooked in soups and flavored with spices, lentils account for a good portion of their protein intake.

Both Fijians and Indians have garden vegetables in their diets. Cabbage, beans, and eggplant are either stewed or cooked in curry. Fijians like taro leaves cooked in coconut cream.

Coconut is a very popular plant in Fiji. Its water is enjoyed as a refreshing beverage, while the grated meat is soaked in boiling water and then squeezed to produce cream or milk. An ecologically destructive dish is millionaire's salad, made from the heart of the coconut tree. To make one salad, a whole mature tree is felled.

The Fijian diet includes increasingly large amounts of canned foods. In many communities, the switch from fresh fruit and vegetables to the canned varieties is a growing cause for concern. Canned beef or sardines have been substituted for fresh meat in many traditional recipes. This reliance on canned foods with excessive fat, sugar, and salt is giving rise to many diseases that were not present in Fiji a few decades ago.

DRINKS

Although very slightly narcotic, kava is an integral part of Fiji's culture. It must be drunk indoors, as drinking alcoholic beverages on the street is prohibited. Strict laws govern the sale of beer and liquor—for example, alcohol cannot be sold on Sundays. The most popular drink, after kava, is Fiji Bitter beer, brewed in Suva and Lautoka.

The national drink of choice is kava. Made by diluting the pounded root of the pepper plant in water, it looks and tastes—to outsiders—like muddy water. Fijians swear that hand-pounded kava tastes better than the machine-ground root. Most of what is available on the market, though, is turned out by machine and sold in small packets for instant mixing with a bowl of water.

There is a wide choice of nonalcoholic beverages. Coconut water is a favorite, while manufactured soda in every flavor is consumed in large quantities. Although fresh fruit is readily available, freshly squeezed fruit juice is not popular. Fijians prefer to drink fruit cordial diluted with water.

MARKETS

Fijians buy their produce from a variety of sources. They can get a few vegetables from an Indian housewife selling garden produce in her front yard or visit the market or supermarket. All the towns have a municipal market as well as a well-stocked supermarket. Villagers are usually self-sufficient in fresh produce.

The Suva Municipal Market is the largest retail produce market in the Pacific. Polynesian, Chinese, Indian, and Fijian vendors sell fish, meat, vegetables, fruit, coconut oil, and nearly everything else that a Fijian household might need. Some vendors sell handicrafts. The ground floor contains all the fresh meats and vegetables, while dried goods are found upstairs. The Indian spices section is a heady mix of aromas and colors. Indian sweets are sold from kiosks at one side of the market. Some of the confections are actually not sweet but spicy.

Large areas are devoted to the sale of kava, whole and ground. A yaqona saloon is dedicated solely to kava drinkers. Passersby are urged to try a bowl by energetic salesmen. Fijian women also sell fresh pineapple and guava juice from glass containers.

Fresh produce is set out on tables at the Suva market.

INTERNET LINKS

https://www.lonelyplanet.com/fiji/travel-tips-and-articles/the -foodies-guide-to-fiji/40625c8c-8a11-5710-a052-1479d2766f50
This travel site provides information on Fijian cuisines for tourists.

https://www.nytimes.com/2018/08/06/t-magazine/polynesian -cuisine.html
This article takes a look at how today's chefs are trying to bring back an authentic Polynesian cuisine.

https://theculturetrip.com/pacific/fiji/articles/flavoursome-fiji -the-best-cuisine-from-the-south-pacific-island
Some of Fiji's most popular dishes are presented on this site.

KOKODA (FIJIAN SPICY FISH)

The raw fish in this iconic Fijian salad is "cooked" in an acidic marinade, much like in a ceviche.

1 pound (450 grams) fresh boneless, skinless
   white fish, such as snapper or mahi
   mahi fillet, cut into ½- to 1-inch (about
   1—2 centimeter) pieces
1 cup (240 mililiters) white vinegar
¾ cup (180 mL) coconut milk
¼ cup (15 g) finely chopped fresh cilantro
3 scallions, thinly sliced
1 tomato, cored, seeded, and finely chopped
1 small red bell pepper, seeded and
   finely chopped
½—1 (according to desired heat) small green
   chile, such as jalepeno or serrano, seeds
   and stem removed, finely chopped
½ small red onion, finely chopped
2 tablespoons fresh lime juice, plus wedges to serve
Kosher salt and freshly ground black pepper

In a large bowl, toss the fish pieces with the white vinegar. Leave to marinate for 30 minutes, then drain and rinse and dry the fish. Return the fish to the bowl along with the coconut milk, cilantro, scallions, tomato, peppers, and red onion, and stir gently to combine. Add the lime juice, salt, and pepper and refrigerate until ready to serve.

SPICED *KUMALA* (SWEET POTATO) AND BANANA SALAD

2 medium sweet potatoes, peeled
4 ripe, medium bananas
1 tablespoon lemon juice
2 Tbsp vegetable oil
2 tsp curry powder
2 cloves garlic, chopped
½ cup (120 mL) mayonnaise
½ cup raisins (optional)
¼ cup green pepper, diced (optional)
2 Tbsp chopped scallions
Salt, black pepper, to taste
Chopped parsley, cilantro, and/or mint

Cut the sweet potatoes into 1-inch (2.5 cm) cubes. Cook in lightly salted boiling water just until tender. Drain the potatoes, and let them cool and dry.

In a small pan, heat oil to medium and lightly sauté the garlic (do not brown); add curry powder and stir just until aromatic. Remove from heat and cool. Stir in the mayonnaise to make a curry dressing.

Slice bananas into a large bowl, and toss with lemon juice. Add the sweet potato, and the raisins and peppers, if using. Fold in the dressing and scallions. Adjust for taste. Garnish with parsley or coriander.

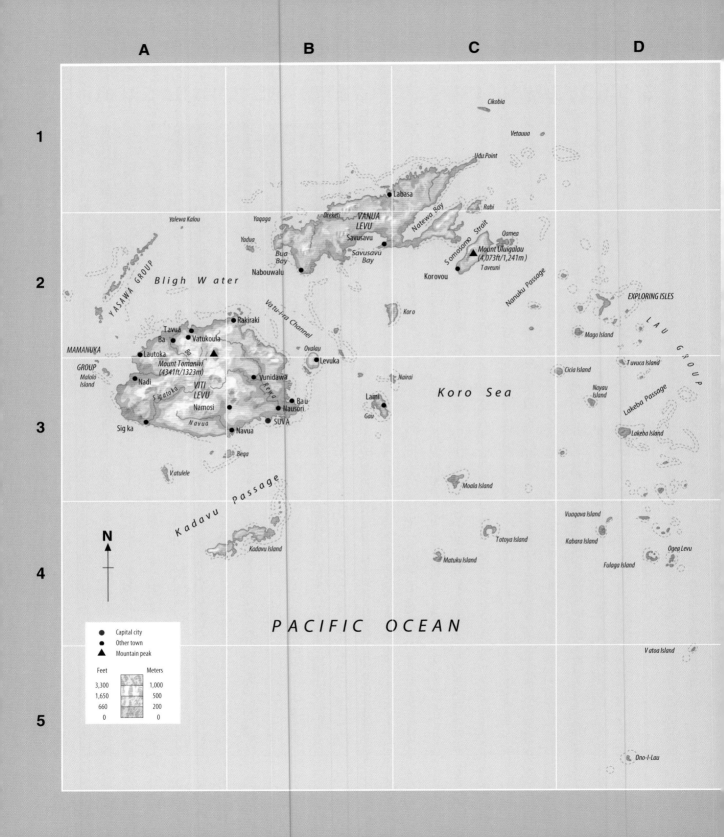

	A	B	C	D

1

Cikobia

Vetauua

Udu Point

Labasa

VANUA LEVU

Dreketi

Yaqaga

Yalewa Kalou

Natewa Bay

Rabi

2

Yadua

Savusavu

Qamea

Bua Bay

Savusavu Bay

Somosomo Strait

Mount Uluigalau
(4,073ft/1,241m)

Nabouwalu

Taveuni

YASAWA GROUP

Bligh Water

Korovou

Nanuku Passage

EXPLORING ISLES

Koro

Mago Island

L A U   G R O U P

Vatu-i-ra Channel

Rakiraki

Tavua

Ba

Vatukoula

MAMANUKA

Lautoka

Mount Tomanivi
(4341ft/1323m)

Ovalau

Levuka

Nairai

Cicia Island

Tuvuca Island

GROUP

Malolo Island

Nadi

VITI LEVU

Vunidawa

Koro Sea

Nayau Island

Sigatoka

Rewa

Lami

Lakeba Passage

Namosi

Bau

Nausori

Gau

3

Sigatoka

Navua

SUVA

Navua

Lakeba Island

Beqa

Vatulele

Moala Island

Kadavu Passage

Vuaqava Island

N

Kadavu Island

Totoya Island

Kabara Island

Ogea Levu

4

Matuku Island

Fulaga Island

PACIFIC OCEAN

	Capital city
●	Other town
▲	Mountain peak

Feet		Meters
3,300		1,000
1,650		500
660		200
0		0

Vatoa Island

5

Ono-I-Lau

MAP OF FIJI

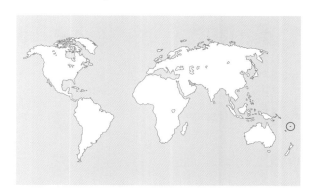

ECONOMIC FIJI

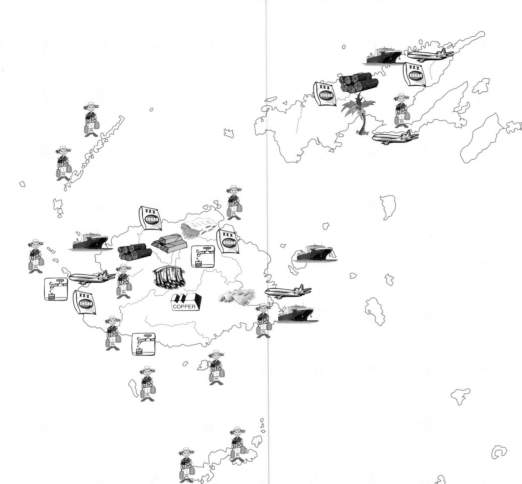

Services

 Airport

 Hydropower

 Ports

 Tourism

Agriculture

 Copra

 Ginger

 Rice

 Sugar

Natural Resources

 Copper

 Gold

 Timber

 Water

ABOUT THE ECONOMY

(all figures are estimates)

GROSS DOMESTIC PRODUCT (GDP)
(Official exchange rate)
$5.079 billion (2017)

GDP PER CAPITA
$9,800 (2017)

CURRENCY
Fiji dollar (FJD)
F$1=100 cents
$1 USD = 2.11 FJD (September 2018)

LABOR FORCE
353,100 (2017)

LABOR FORCE BY OCCUPATION
Agriculture: 44.2 percent
Industry: 14.3 percent
Services: 41.6 percent (2011)

UNEMPLOYMENT RATE
5.5 percent (2017)

POPULATION BELOW POVERTY LINE
31 percent (2009)

INFLATION
3.4 percent (2017)

NATURAL RESOURCES
Timber, gold, silver, copper, fish, beaches, hydropower, potential offshore oil

AGRICULTURAL PRODUCTS
Sugar, timber, copra, coconut oil, root crops, rice, fruits and vegetables, ginger

MAIN INDUSTRIES
Tourism, sugar, clothing, copra, gold, silver, lumber

MAIN EXPORTS
Fuel (including oil), fish, beverages, gems, sugar, garments, gold, timber, fish, molasses, coconut oil, mineral water

MAIN IMPORTS
Manufactured goods, machinery and transport equipment, petroleum products, food and beverages, chemicals, tobacco

MAIN TRADE PARTNERS
Australia, New Zealand, United States, Singapore, China

CULTURAL FIJI

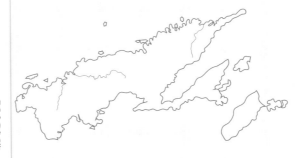

Momi Gun Battery
Built in 1941 to protect Fiji from a possible Japanese invasion, the battery contains two six-inch guns, one of which is rumored to have been used in the Boer War and the other during World War I.

Navala Village
The last remaining thatched-hut village in Fiji decided in 1950 to reject modern building materials. All youth are encouraged to learn the traditional art of bure making.

Cession Site
Here King Cakobau signed the Deed of Cession in 1874, handing over the sovereignty of Fiji to Great Britain as well as his iconic war club.

Garden of the Sleeping Giant
Originally designed to house actor Raymond Burr's private collection of tropical orchids, the garden showcases over two thousand different varieties of orchids, covering 50 acres (20 ha).

Tavuni Hill Fort
Built by a Tongan chief in the eighteenth century, this best example of a traditional Fijian fort offers a glimpse into what war was like in olden times. Restored exhibits include cooking ovens, waste pits, and even a killing stone.

Sigatoka Sand Dunes
Stretching over several miles, these dunes were an ancient burial ground. Archaeological findings include Lapita pottery.

Laucala Ring-Ditch Fort
The fort was built in the eighteenth century to protect the settlement from people migrating from the interior. The site is unique for its double fortification—two ring-ditch forts side by side.

Fiji Museum
The best museum in Fiji displays a double-hulled war canoe in its grand hall. Other exhibits include cannibal forks, war clubs, and tattooing tools. The Indo-Fijian Gallery recounts the history of Indian indentured laborers brought to Fiji.

ABOUT THE CULTURE

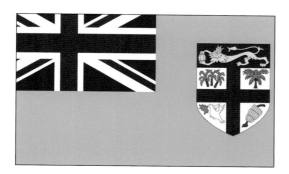

(all figures are estimates)

OFFICIAL NAME
Republic of Fiji

GOVERNMENT TYPE
Parliamentary republic

CAPITAL
Suva (on Viti Levu)

MAJOR CITIES
Suva, Nadi, Lautoka, Nausori, Sigatoka, Levuka, Labasa, Savusavu

PROVINCES
One dependency, Rotuma, and fourteen provinces: Ba, Bua, Cakaudrove, Kadavu, Lau, Lomaiviti, Macuata, Nadroga-Navosa, Naitasiri, Namosi, Ra, Rewa, Serua, Tailevu

POPULATION
920,938 (2017)

URBAN POPULATION
56.2 percent (2018)

RELIGIONS
Christian (64.7 percent), Hindu (27.9 percent), Muslim (6.3 percent), Sikh (0.3 percent), others or none (0.8 percent) (2007)

ETHNIC GROUPS
iTaukei 56.8 percent (predominantly Melanesian with a Polynesian admixture), Indian 37.5 percent, Rotuman 1.2 percent, other 4.5 percent (European, part European, other Pacific Islanders, Chinese) (2007)
Note: a 2010 law replaces "Fijian" with "iTaukei" when referring to the original and native settlers of Fiji

LANGUAGES
English (official), Fijian (official), Hindi

LIFE EXPECTANCY AT BIRTH
Total population: 73 years
Male: 70.3 years
Female: 75.8 years (2017)

INFANT MORTALITY RATE
9.5 deaths per 1,000 live births (2015)

FERTILITY RATE
2.65 children born per woman (2009 estimate)

TIMELINE

IN FIJI	IN THE WORLD
1000 BCE	
Austronesian settlers arrive from the west.	
1300–1800s CE	**1206–1368**
Tongan incursions from the east. Dutch seafarer Abel Tasman sights Vanua Levu.	Genghis Khan unifies the Mongols and starts conquest of the world.
1774	
Captain James Cook visits Vatoa.	**1776**
1822	US Declaration of Independence signed.
European settlement begins at Levuka.	
1830	
First Christian missionaries arrive at Lakeba.	
1853	
Cakobau installed as high chief of Bau.	**1861**
1867	The US Civil War begins.
Unrest grows; Cakobau becomes king of Bau; Rev. Thomas Baker is eaten by cannibals.	
1868	
Polynesia Company buys Suva in exchange for paying Cakobau's debts.	**1869**
1871	The Suez Canal is opened.
Central government formed at Levuka, makes Cakobau king of Fiji.	
1874	
Cakobau's government collapses; cedes Fiji to Britain without a price tag.	
1875	
Sir Arthur Gordon becomes first governor of Fiji.	
1879	
First Indians arrive as indentured laborers.	
1882	
Capital moved from Levuka to Suva.	
	1914
1916	World War I begins.
Recruitment of indentured labor ends.	
1917–1918	
Fijian soldiers support Allies in World War I.	
1942–1945	**1945**
Fijians excel as jungle scouts with Allied military in World War II.	The United States drops atomic bombs on Hiroshima and Nagasaki, Japan. World War II ends.

IN FIJI	IN THE WORLD
1966 Fijian-dominated Alliance Party wins Fiji's first elections.	
1970 Fiji becomes independent; Ratu Sir Kamisese Mara chosen as first prime minister.	
	1986 Nuclear power disaster at Chernobyl in Ukraine.
1987 Fijian-Indian coalition wins majority in election. Sitiveni Rabuka stages two bloodless military coups.	
	1991 Breakup of the Soviet Union.
1992 Rabuka's party wins election, making him prime minister.	
	1997 Hong Kong is returned to China.
1999 Mahendra Chaudhry elected Fiji's first Indian prime minister.	
2000 George Speight leads coup and takes the cabinet hostage.	
2001 Laisenia Qarase wins majority in new elections.	**2001** Terrorists attack the United States on September 11.
2002 Speight found guilty of treason, sentenced to life imprisonment.	**2003** War in Iraq begins.
2006 Army chief Frank Bainimarama overthrows Qarase and installs Chaudhry as finance minister.	
2007 Bainimarama appointed interim prime minister.	**2008** The first black president of the United States, Barack Obama, is elected.
2009 The Commonwealth suspends Fiji.	
2014 Elections held, Bainimarama reelected; Commonwealth reinstates Fiji as a full member.	
2016 Cyclone Winston hits Fiji in the worst storm ever recorded in the Southern Hemisphere. Fiji Rugby Sevens win gold medal at Summer Olympics.	**2015–2016** ISIS launches terror attacks in Belgium and France.
2018 General elections held November 14.	**2017** Donald Trump becomes US president.
	2018 Winter Olympics in South Korea

GLOSSARY

bilo (MBIH-loh)
A bowl made from half a coconut shell.

bula **(MBU-lah)**
A common Fijian greeting, meaning "life."

bure **(MB00-reh)**
A traditional Fijian thatched dwelling.

choli **(CHOH-lih)**
A short, tight blouse worn with the sari by Indian women.

dhoti
A white loincloth worn by Indian men.

kava
A slightly sedating drink made from the dried roots of the pepper plant.

kerekere **(kay-reh-KAY-ray)**
A Fijian folkway of seeking favors from relatives.

lovo **(LOH-voh)**
A feast cooked by hot stones in a covered underground pit also called lovo.

masi **(MAH-sih)**
A traditional pounded bark cloth with a smooth and feltlike finish.

mataqali **(mah-tang-GAH-lee)**
An extended family group.

meke **(MAY-keh)**
A traditional performance combining song, dance, and theater.

roti
A flat tortilla-like bread made of wheat flour and cooked on a griddle.

sari
A traditional garment of Indian women, worn as a full, wraparound skirt with one end draped over the left shoulder.

sulu **(SOO-loo)**
A wraparound skirt worn by adults, short for men and long for women.

tabla
An Indian drum played in pairs.

tabua **(TAM-bwah)**
A polished whale tooth used as a diplomatic gift in traditional society.

tanoa **(TAH-nwah)**
A large wooden bowl for ceremonial mixing of kava.

vakalolo **(vah-kah-LOH-loh)**
A sweet pudding of cassava, taro, and breadfruit.

yaqona **(yang-GOH-nah)**
An elaborate ceremony for drinking kava.

FOR FURTHER INFORMATION

BOOKS

Hajratwala, Minal. *Moon Fiji*. 10th ed. Berkley, CA: Moon Travel, 2019.

Lutwick, Will. *Dodging Machetes: How I Survived Forbidden Love, Bad Behavior, and the Peace Corps in Fiji*. Oakland, CA: Peace Corps Writers, 2012.

Ryan, Ben. *Sevens Heaven: The Beautiful Chaos of Fiji's Olympic Dream*. London: Weidenfeld & Nicolson, 2018.

WEBSITES

BBC News, Fiji Country Profile. https://www.bbc.com/news/world-asia-pacific-14919067

BBC News, Fiji Timeline. https://www.bbc.com/news/world-asia-pacific-14919688

CIA World Factbook, Fiji. https://www.cia.gov/library/publications/the-world-factbook/geos/fj.html

Fijian Government. http://www.fiji.gov.fj

Fiji Times. https://www.fijitimes.com

New York Times. "Fiji News and Archives." https://www.nytimes.com/topic/destination/fiji

FILMS

Fiji Firewalkers. Tom Vendetti. Vendetti Productions, 2006.

The Land Has Eyes. Vilsoni Hereniko. 2004.

MUSIC

Various Artists. *Fiji: Independence Day.* Blind Man Sound, 2007.

Various Artists. *Fiji: Indigenous Life.* Indigenous Alliance, 2008.

Various Artists. *Fiji: Xperience.* Blind Man Sound, 2007.

Various Artists. *Music of the Fiji Islands.* Arc Music, 2005.

BIBLIOGRAPHY

"Fiji." CIA World Factbook. https://www.cia.gov/library/publications/the-world-factbook/geos/fj.html.

"Fiji." *Encyclopaedia Britannica*. https://www.britannica.com/place/Fiji-republic -Pacific-Ocean.

Fiji Times. http://www.fijitimes.com

Jones, Catherine, Warwick E. Murray, and John Overton. "FIJI Water, Water Everywhere: Global Brands and Democratic and Social Injustice." *Asia Pacific Viewpoint*, February 2017. Wiley Online Library. https://onlinelibrary.wiley.com/doi/full/10.1111/apv.12144

Kitson, Robert. "Fiji Waltz to Olympic Rugby Sevens Gold Against Outclassed Great Britain." *Guardian*, August 11, 2016. https://www.theguardian.com/sport/2016/aug/11/fiji-great-britain-rio-2016-rugby-sevens-final

Prasad, Rajendra. "Banished and Excluded: The Girmit of Fiji." *Himal Southasian,* January 2, 2015. http://himalmag.com/girmit-fiji.

Schwartz, Dominque. "Fiji Fishermen Warn Foreign Boats Over-Fishing in Pacific Destroying Local Tuna Industry." Australian Broadcasting Corporation News, April 2014. http://www.abc.net.au/news/2014-04-19/an-fiji-fishing-crisis/5399692

Solomon, Serena. "Counting on the Trendy to Revive Kava, a Traditional Drink." *New York Times*, February 23, 2017. https://www.nytimes.com/2017/02/23/business/fiji-kava -prices-drink.html

Statista. "Sales of the Leading Bottled Still Water Brands in the United States in 2017 (in Million US Dollars)." https://www.statista.com/statistics/188312/top-bottled-still-water -brands-in-the-united-states

United Nations Development Programme. "Human Development Reports." http://hdr.undp.org/en/composite/HDI

Vula, Maraia. "Coconut Industry's Future Bright: Pillay." *Fiji Sun*, March 23, 2018. https://www.pressreader.com/fiji/fiji-sun/20180323/282114932115368

World Health Organization. "Fiji: WHO Statistical Profile." http://www.who.int/gho/countries/fji.pdf

World Travel & Tourism Council. "Travel & Tourism Economic Impact 2017 Fiji." https://www.wttc.org/-/media/files/reports/economic-impact-research/countries-2017/fiji2017.pdf

INDEX

INDEX